Fred Walker.

THE POWER

OF BALANCE

A Rolfing View of Health

by

Brian W. Fahey, Ph.D.

Published by

METAMORPHOUS PRESS
P.O. Box 10616
Portland, Oregon 97210

Library of Congress Cataloging-in-Publication Data

Fahey, Brian W.
   The power of balance: a Rolfing view of health / by Brian W. Fahey.
     p.   cm.
   Bibliography: p.

   ISBN 0-943920-52-3
   1. Rolfing.   I. Title.
RC489.R64F35   1988
615.8'22 – dc 19   88-1536
                                   CIP

Cover Art by Penland Guertsch
Illustrations by Stanley K. Lester

Typesetting by Cy-Ann Designs, Portland, Oregon
Printed in U.S.A.

"New times, they say, require new remedies. New times also demand and consequently receive new forms, new ideas, perhaps a new man. One of the pregnant ideas of this decade is that human behavior is basically an outward and visible functional response of structural organization or the lack thereof."

Ida P. Rolf, Ph.D.

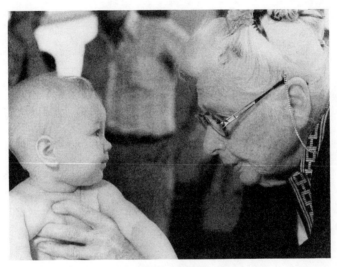

IDA P. ROLF
May 19, 1896 — New York, N.Y.
March 19, 1979 — Bryn Mawr, PA

"Humans have always developed and still live within the gravity pull of the earth. They must make peace with this energy field, whatever it really is. To the extent that they fail to make peace and mistakenly carry on war, gravity wins every time. The energy of this field can enhance or dissipate the energy of the individual man. You cannot change the energy field, but you can change the man."

ACKNOWLEDGEMENTS

I am very grateful to my friend and Rolfing teacher Jan Sultan for contributing so much to my understanding of the Rolfing work which fills the pages of this book. I am eternally thankful for the unwavering love and support that my wife Gail has provided during the long process of bringing this work to completion. My beautiful children Caitlin and Ravenna inspire me more than I could ever express adequately. I am deeply grateful for my father and mother, Howard and Leona Fahey, for instilling in me the values of integrity, determination, and consistency which have carried me through a very meaningful life. I am very happy to be associated with Victor Roberge and the competent and considerate staff at Metamorphous Press. Finally, I tip my hat once again to Ida P. Rolf, whose germinal ideas form the foundation of this work and whose persistent spirit encourages me daily as I glance at her picture on the wall in my Rolfing room.

Brian W. Fahey, Ph.D.
Albuquerque, NM

TABLE OF CONTENTS

PREFACE
The Body Loves Balance

This is the gospel of Rolfing: When the body gets working appropriately, the force of gravity can flow through. Then, spontaneously, the body heals itself.

I.P.R.

This is a book about the importance of balance in all aspects of life. It expands upon the original ideas about improving health by balancing body structure first developed by Ida P. Rolf, Ph.D. Dr. Rolf, formerly a biochemist with the Rockefeller Institute (now Rockefeller University in New York City), developed a system of direct body manipulation and education known as Structural Integration, or "Rolfing".[1] As early as the 1930s, Dr. Rolf was regularly "rolling up her sleeves" and using her talents of direct physical manipulation to help people with various structural disorders. Painter Georgia O'Keefe relates that in 1938 Ida used to come to her New York apartment to give her "body treatments." The political climate at this time was somewhat repressive towards "natural therapies." The fledgling American Medical Association was attempting to lobby for strict regulations governing chiropractic, osteopathic, naturopathic, and homeopathic practitioners. Dr. Rolf's ideas for improving human *function* by organizing

---

1. See *Ida Rolf Talks About Rolfing and Physical Reality,* Rosemary Feitis, Harper and Row, 1978, and *Rolfing: The Integration of Human Structures, Ida P. Rolf,* Dennis Landman, 1977.

body *structure* were also met with scepticism by the medical hierarchy. A woman of tremendous determination, she persevered with her work and was invited to England to share her ideas and methods with some members of the British Osteopathic community. She later returned to the United States and continued her research and did body work on those who found their way to her door in increasing numbers. Rolf was convinced of the incredible power of human touch and she knew her unique views of structure, gravity, and connective tissues forming the framework of focused touch, had great healing potential. Her work received a great boost of notoriety in the 1960s when she was invited west to lecture and do body work at Esalen Institute, a "growth center" in Big Sur, California. At this point people began to request training in Rolf's work. This eventually led to the establishment of a sequential training program and permanent teaching facility in Boulder, Colorado. In retrospect, Ida Rolf can be viewed as a diligent worker, a gutsy pioneer who guided her ideas and methods through very difficult times. The author is very grateful for Ida Rolf's genius and her determination to see the ideas through to demonstrable results.

Rolfing consists of a series of ten sessions of body work, lasting about an hour each and usually spaced a week apart. The manipulation proceeds from the surface of the body, alternating between the upper and lower halves while moving toward deeper levels. Rolfing releases local areas of stress and tightness, and also reorganizes major body segments (head, torso, pelvis and legs) into a more efficient energy system.

Almost everyone is concerned with good posture. From the Rolfing perspective, "posture" is a surface condition. A person's posture and movement patterns reflect the state of their underlying structure. Good posture is not created through holding and effort, but by releasing restricted areas and allowing the body to operate with ease and grace. Everything we think, say, and do will either add to or decrease the level of order and balance in our bodies and in our lives. This book suggests how you can take a more active role in creating balance and elevating your level of well-being.

We've all heard plenty about the impending energy crisis in fuels and other natural resources. This book examines an equally important crisis, on a more personal level — the blocking of energy in the human body caused by accumulated stress which results in structural disorder. When people's bodies get stuck, they also tend to get bogged down in negative patterns of thinking and feeling. This state reduces our efficiency and begins to show up as physical aches and pains. If the imbalanced patterns continue, the person will begin to experience symptoms with medical labels like "colitis," "arthritis," "high blood pressure," "back trouble," and "migraine headaches," to name a few. To a Rolfer, these stress-related symptoms indicate imbalance in the entire musculo-skeletal system.

Rolfing will benefit people who seemingly have no visible "symptoms" as well as those who have specific structural problems (spinal curvature, bow legs, chronic low back pain, etc.) The slightest structural misalignment can have a profound impact on a person, whether it is consciously recognized or not. Rolfers are continuously amazed at how the most minute change in body alignment can have an enormous effect on a person's attitude and the way they carry themselves. Rolfers feel that the creation of an inner experience of balance is equally important as "fixing" a person's visible signs of disorder. Before being Rolfed, most people have a sense of "using" their body as a tool and experience it in a very generalized way. Rolfing connects body and consciousness, giving a person access to a more subtle and integrated awareness of being themselves.

The Rolfing process educates, reorganizes, and balances the body into an integrated system. The balance achieved from Rolfing works its way through the whole system to improve our level of health. It is the premise of this book that balanced bodies (people) are more creative, sensitive, powerful, and emotionally secure than their unbalanced peers. Rolfing removes obstructions which keep bodies from following their natural desire to achieve balance.

Rolfing also involves the study of body *structure* with an eye for its ideal *function*, which leads to new information about its optimal *design*. The results from this study are guidelines for ordered development for babies, children, or adults. Rolfing ideas can be applied to all aspects of daily life, including how we sit, stand, walk, do our jobs, play, and ultimately, how we feel about ourselves. Reading this book can be a step toward achieving a high level of structural balance, energy, and well-being for yourself.

"If you would see a person's soul, look at his body."[2]

Brian W. Fahey, Ph.D.
Albuquerque, NM

---

2.   Alice Steadman, *Who's The Matter With Me,* De Vorss & Co. 1966, p. 3.

1

WHAT IS ROLFING?

Rolfers make a life study of relating bodies and their fields to the earth and its gravity field, and we so organize the body that the gravity field can reinforce the body's energy field. This is our primary concept.[1]

Rolfing[2] is a system of manipulation designed to re-balance the body by bringing its major segments — head, shoulders, chest, pelvis and legs — into vertical alignment. Ida P. Rolf, Ph.D., formerly an organic chemist with the Rockefeller Institute, developed this process after many years of study and practical experimentation. She saw that poor alignment was the major cause of gravitational stress on the body. Conversely, she believed that same gravity could promote balance and ease stress if a body was in proper relationship with it.

Someone who practices the art of Rolfing is called a Rolfer. Rolfers are trained to see how a person's body structure is organized and how it moves through space. The Rolfer is concerned with such things as the relationship between the upper and lower halves of the body. Can the legs support the pelvis and does the pelvis support the

---

1. All quotes at the beginning of each chapter come from *Ida Rolf Talks About Rolfing and Physical Reality*, edited and with an Introduction by Rosemary Feitis, Rolf Institute, Boulder, Colorado 1978.
2. The word "Rolfing" is a Service Mark of the Rolf Institute of Structural Integration, Boulder, Colorado.

torso and neck? Do the left and right sides of the body match? Do the front and back surfaces of the body support each other in movement? Are the inner and outer surfaces of the body related well to each other? When the body is balanced in all these respects, it functions better and the person feels better.

Through direct manipulation of the connective tissues, the Rolfer helps to establish more order in the body and then the body is more at ease in gravity. Connective tissues include ligaments, tendons, and fascia. Thin sheets of fascia are wrapped around all of our muscles and organs. The connective tissues work together to give the body its internal form and external shape. Connective tissues are very pliable and can be molded into many shapes, like clay. This pliable quality of connective tissues can work for or against body alignment, just as gravity can become a supporting influence for a balanced body, or a stressful force on an imbalanced or misaligned body. Accidents, surgery, emotional traumas, and the way a person sits, stands, and walks can mold the connective tissues into hardened patterns. A person literally becomes "stuck" in a characteristic pattern that is uniquely their own. Rolfing takes advantage of the pliable quality of the connective tissues. The Rolfer applies pressure with his hands to the hardened tissues. This allows fluids to move out of the congested areas, so tissues can regain their normal tone and proper positioning in the body. The Rolfer works in all tissue levels, from surface to deep, in concert with the client's ability to release. He or she applies only the pressure necessary to reorganize tissue. Pain may occur intermittently during sessions. The degree will vary according to such things as the duration and intensity of manipulation in a particularly contracted area, one's tolerance of and interpretation of sensation, one's conscious or unconscious resistance to change, and the awareness and tension level in the Rolfer's body as he or she works. As chronic tension is often caused by emotional stress, some feelings of pain may accompany emotional as well as physical release.

People come to be Rolfed for a variety of reasons. Generally, they can be classified into three categories:

(a) People who use and want to understand their bodies more fully, such as dancers, coaches and teachers of movement, and athletes, from recreational to professional levels.

(b) People in chronic pain resulting from injury or from recurring trouble spots in their body, such as migraine headaches, low back pain, knee weaknesses and neck and shoulder tension. If you consider the following statistics you can see how important an effective solution to lower back and neck problems could become to the nation's health problems:

1) In 1985 75 million Americans suffered some form of back ailment.
2) Two point five (2.5) million Americans are totally disabled from back conditions.
3) There are more than 200,000 surgeries per year for back problems.
4) Back problems are the leading cause of absenteeism and disability with a cost to industry estimated at $14 billion dollars a year.
5) Back problems are the second leading cause of hopsitalization (pregnancy is first).
6) Back ailments are responsible for 18 million doctor visits a year.
7) Back problems cost 93 million work days annually.

(c) People who want to expand their potential by becoming aware of and releasing blocked emotional and structural patterns which inhibit their sense of well-being.

The objective visual results of Rolfing include improved posture (structure). The soles of the feet meet the ground more squarely, the knees and feet track more forward and parallel, the torso is more balanced on the pelvis, and the head and neck are more balanced on the torso. The overall appearance of the body is lighter and longer. The subjective, experiential changes vary greatly from person to person. Generally, people report feeling lighter and moving more efficiently, a sense that their joints are "well oiled." They experience a release of chronic pain conditions, an increase in energy, and they feel released from the patterns that create chronic stress and tensions. They experience heightened self-awareness, new ease in interpersonal communications, and a more positive self image. Separately, or in conjunction with their Rolfing, many clients will work with a Certified Rolfing Movement teacher, trained to help people find ways to better utilize their bodies in movement. This work strongly enhances the changes in body structure and function begun by the Rolfing manipulation.[3]

A typical first visit to a Rolfer could proceed as follows: After taking a short physical history, the Rolfer will observe and photograph the client (dressed in underwear) from front, back, and side views, to see how balanced their body is in a standing position. The client may then be asked to walk or get in and out of a chair so the Rolfer can observe how their body functions while moving. The Rolfer will identify areas of existing tension and strain and perhaps point out where future trouble spots may develop.

3.   See Appendix B for a full discussion of Rolfing Movement Integration.

Rolfing is not a medical treatment. Rolfers are concerned with the overall pattern of the body, the way it "stacks up" in the gravity field. (Figures 1 and 2) After the evaluation, the client lies on a padded table while the Rolfer touches his or her body to feel for areas of tension and distress. The Rolfer will use fingers, knuckles, and maybe an occasional elbow, pressing and stretching the body to begin loosening the bound-up connective tissues. Initially, Rolfing involves a carefully planned sequence of ten sessions,

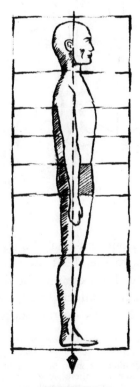

FIGURE 1
Rolfers are concerned with the overall pattern of the body, the way it "stacks up" in the gravity field.

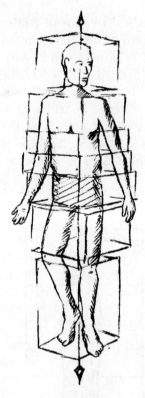

FIGURE 2

each lasting one to one-and-a-half hours.[4] In each session the Rolfer works with the client on a different body area, depth, and function. For example, the first session focuses on the chest, ribs, and shoulders to improve breathing. The second session could work on the knees, feet and legs to

4.   Rolfing offers a continuing program of health maintenance and improvement. In addition to sessions 1-10 there are sessions 11-15, sometimes called Advanced Sessions, which continue the development started in the basic sequence. "Tune up" sessions work in specific areas that the client needs help in and "First Aid" sessions help in the rehabilitation process following an accident or injury.

create the resilience needed to balance future changes elsewhere in the body. Constricted areas are released, circulation is improved, and the client gains awareness of overall body balance. Unlike massage, the Rolfing process will actually change relationships between body parts, creating a structure that more comfortably reflects the individual. You don't have to be injured or in a chronic condition to benefit significantly from Rolfing. Most of us experience our bodies in such generalized ways that we have no idea how the most delicate imbalances can disrupt our ease and affect our attitudes. Even the slightest shift in alignment can reduce our level of aliveness and begin a pattern of stressful compensation. If we aren't in tune with our bodies we may not even realize the extent to which we are out of balance until we are "hit in the face" with a very definite symptom. The slightest misalignment could be what is holding us back from realizing our full potential.

The body flexes (contracts) in order to hold onto or not deal with particular attitudes and emotions. If this pattern can be eased slightly, the person has a chance to release the emotion and can explore new ways of experiencing themselves and the world. Softening parts of the structure can soften attitudes and habitual ways of behaving. I am continuously amazed by behavioral changes. Often, after only one session, a person's shoulders relax and their hiked-up chest drops. The next time they come for a session, their attitude and the way they express themselves has already begun to change. After some Rolfing sessions, a 34 year old professional dancer commented

"I realized that the pride I carried was a false pride, a way of keeping me from truly knowing myself and from allowing others to see my softer side."

Physicians frequently refer their patients to Rolfers to assist in post-operative recovery or as an adjunct to traditional physical therapy. Other times, a person will see a Rolfer independently and then request a doctor's support in the form of a recommendation so that insurance can help with the fees. Also, more and more parents are bringing their young children to be Rolfed. They realize that structural patterns can be changed more easily when they have had less time to develop. Children usually need fewer sessions than adults as they have not had enough time to fuse structure and character as tightly.

All Rolfers are certified by the Rolf Institute of Structural Integration in Boulder, Colorado. The Institute facilitates ongoing research on the effects of Rolfing and the Rolfing Movement work, as well as a program of continuing education for certified Rolfers. In 1981, the Rolf Institute brought its training program to the European continent and since then has been conducting Rolfing Training classes in Europe with the Institute's representative office administering Rolfing activities in Munich, West Germany. Generally two classes each year are taught in Europe (usually in Munich). These classes are sanctioned by the Rolf Institute and are taught by Rolf Institute Instructors. Upon completion of training in Europe, individuals receive certification from the Rolf Institute's International Headquarters in Boulder, Colorado. Currently there are approximately 60 certified Rolfers and Movement Teachers on the European continent. In addition to Europe, the Rolf Institute is expanding its training program to Brazil where there is currently a group of approximately ten certified Rolfers. Continuing Education workshops are being conducted in Brazil and it is anticipated within the next few years Rolfing Training Classes for beginning students will be taught in Brazil. For a list of certified Rolfers and more information about Rolfing, please send inquiries to:

Richard A. Stenstadvold, Managing Director
Rolf Institute
P.O. Box 1868
Boulder, Colorado 80306
(303) 449-5903

2

SELF FORMATION
Our Journey Through The Flesh

A child may grow bigger, but as long as he's still stuck in the same child form is it surprising that he should be stuck in his same emotional child thing? It's worked for him for a long, long time. How does he know that anything else is going to work any better? How does he have any motivation to get out of it? The more you watch people change in front of your eyes, the more sure you are about how people can get stuck in childish incidents, or birth incidents, or for all I know pre-birth incidents.

I.P.R.

How do bodies get out of balance in the first place? The answer can be found by examining how we develop in and adapt to our environment. This chapter explores some of the influences we must contend with as we move through life, our journey through the flesh. We live within two major boundaries. The first is conception, the meeting of sperm and ova in a fertile environment. Here life is nourished and protected until it can enter the world. The final event is death, in which the body is no longer capable of maintaining itself in the world.

Time, genetic inheritance, and personal experience combine to create the unique flavor of each individual life. Our genes provide the basic blueprint for our development. Body type, hair, eye and skin color are all coded into our cells. We also inherit certain strengths and shortcomings.

The vast data bank of possibilities in our genes provides
the raw material which is shaped by our unique experience
in life. Once a genetic "choice" is made we build on it and
develop around it. This choice then becomes the reality
with which we live. We are uniquely shaped by life experience, including patterns of emotional distress, type and
frequency of physical contact, quality of nutrition, and
conscious and subconscious feelings about the body (received from parents, peers, and media), to name a few. The
extent to which each of these factors alters body structure
will vary greatly from person to person, but combined,
they do influence the shape and balance of our bodies. In
the discussion of life as a journey, five phases will be covered which generally bracket our experiences: conception,
birth, childhood/adolescence, adulthood, and full maturity.

CONCEPTION

It is becoming increasingly probable for me to believe
that a person's fundamental sense of body-self may be
shaped by the events surrounding conception. The physical
and emotional state of the parents sets the stage. Is the
pregnancy a wanted one? Is it a surprise or a planned event?
If there is an unexpected and unwanted pregnancy, should
there be an abortion? Does the mother have a well-balanced
body? Any distress in the mother can be registered by the
embryo. A Rolf client, who I'll call Mary, is a successful
account executive for a radio station. When Mary was
twenty-five she found out that her conception was not
planned. Her real father (her mother has since divorced
and remarried) wanted the pregnancy aborted. She said

"There has always been this sense of anxiety and un-
easiness that I felt, but could never find reasons for. The
day my mother told me that I was an 'accident' I knew

right away where many of my insecure feelings had come from."

If the father does not want the child, the mother will react to his negativity emotionally and physically by releasing stress chemicals and contracting in her body. Because the blood supplies of the mother and child "intermingle", the child will receive these chemical messages. Although it does not intellectually understand the stress, the fetus does "contract" in response to it. Years later, an adult's structure and posture may express this distress. The child's body has recorded the feeling of being unwanted as tension and muscular rigidity. During a particularly emotional session of Rolfing, John, who was adopted when he was three years old, related the following:

"From a very early age I had this gut sense that I wasn't wanted by my real parents. I've always thought of someday finding them and asking them why they got rid of me."

The point to be made here is that these emotional states will create a corresponding physical reaction that will forever "flavor" a person's experience of their body.

The quality of nutritional intake and the degree of structural balance of the mother will strongly affect the child's well-being. As we are forming, we are easily affected by our mother's smoking, alcohol intake, drug use or abuse and, to some extent, the actual form of her body structure. If the mother is well-nourished and happy, the likelihood increases that her body will be a welcome environment. If the form of her body is imbalanced, i.e. a rotation in the pelvis, the child has to adapt to the available space as she grows. This adaptation may include growing into a form not completely in accord with the original "blueprint." Sally is a very competitive, independent and athletic woman. When she became pregnant with Jason she was determined "not to let the pregnancy get in my way." She continued to exercise vigorously, running ten miles a day until three and a half weeks before Jason's birth. She only gained sixteen pounds during the pregnancy and felt flattered when people said she "hardly looked pregnant at all." Jason weighed five pounds, three ounces at birth. Sally's labor was long and difficult, and forceps finally had to be used to bring Jason out. The baby's torso was very short and compressed compared to his long arms and legs because there was so little room in his cramped growing quarters. The cranium showed very noticeable compression and torsion. Fortunately, a friend told Sally about Rolfing one month after his birth. Both she and Jason came in for Rolfing sessions. Jason's torso and spine lengthened, and he and his mom released much tension as their bodies moved toward a more flexible and balanced state. The body work gave each a fresh start as the imprinted trauma of gestation and birth was released.

BIRTH

Birth can be an easy and natural process, or a trauma leaving lasting scars on body and character.[1,2] The attitude of those present, the length of labor, the nature of presentation, the type of medical intervention (if any) and post birth care of the child are all factors that combine to determine the quality of the birth experience. It is amazing how often clients discuss the events of their birth and early childhood (things they never remembered before) while

---

1.   Viola Fryman, D.O., "The Trauma of Birth" in Cranial Concepts and Therapy, Osteopathic Annals, pp. 8-14.
2.   Thomas Vernay, *Secret Life of The Unborn Child*, Summit Books, NY, NY, 1981.

they are being Rolfed. I find more and more that these
early experiences significantly shape one's sense of self and
feelings about life.

Historically, the big question was "will the mother and
child survive the experience?" Now, as our understanding
and technology have improved, the quality of the birth as·
a factor in well-being has become an important consideration. Spinal blocks, Caesarean sections, electronic monitoring devices, and forceps delivery create trauma for both
mother and child. Breech and face presentation are examples of "abnormal" entries into the world that can significantly alter body structure. It is interesting to note that
the clients I see who were delivered with forceps will frequently have cranial problems such as headaches, vision
problems, facial asymmetry, and jaw, neck, and shoulder
pain from imbalances in the biting surfaces of their teeth.
Those who were breech seem to have problems in their
pelvis and low back and at the junction of shoulder to
neck and neck to head.

Consider these statistics — 95% of all births in U.S.
hospitals are medicated in some way.[3] That's 3.5 million
out of 3.7 million births a year. Pain killing and anesthetic
drugs routinely given to American women during childbirth can cause damage to their babies — particularly their
thinking ability, motor skills, and behavior.[4] This is not to
say that the application of technology to childbirth is
not necessary and desirable at times. What I am pointing
out is that the natural process of birth is routinely treated
as a surgical emergency by the majority of the medical
community. In most hospital births, the child is brought
into a strange environment with intense visual, auditory,

3.   East West Journal, July 1979.
4.   More recent data suggest this percentage to now be more near 76% to
82% as more people are requesting non-medicated births. The point is that
birth is still viewed as a medical event rather than a normal occurrence.

and tactile sensations and usually taken away from their mother to a nursery of other crying babies. This kind of reception may create flexion and emotional withdrawal in a newborn. Such flexive reactions create structural imbalance, and may often develop into symptoms in later life. Birth is a uniquely receptive state as the baby's sensory system is wide open. Imprinting of the quality of this experience is unavoidable. We must do more to make this first experience of the world as safe and sensitive as possible.

"What makes being born so frightful is the intensity of the experience, its suffocating richness . . . Birth is a tidal wave of sensation, surpassing anything we can imagine. This is birth, the torture of an innocent. What futility to believe that so great a cataclysm will not leave its mark."[5]

CHILDHOOD / ADOLESCENCE

There are many things that may have a detrimental effect on a child's body structure during infancy. Excessively heavy diapers, or always carrying an infant astride the same hip, can force the legs wider apart than they should be. This will cause the child to adapt at both the pelvis and lower leg as he starts to walk. You might expect to see turned-in or ducked-out feet or a sway back as a result. Too early walking or sitting can also cause problems in the legs and pelvis. Muscles and bones that get pressed into service before they are adequately developed to support this kind of movement will often deform under the extra strain. (Figures 3 and 4) "Potty training" can be

5.   Frederic LeBoyer, *Birth Without Violence*, Alfred A. Knopf, 1978.

FIGURE 3
Extra diapers may force a child to "walk around" it's pelvis, further reinforcing pelvic misalignment and gait pattern.

FIGURE 4
Structural patterns are set into the body very early in life. Carrying a child astride the same hip can cause structural adaptation and imbalance for both mother and child.

traumatic for a child because of the strong negative over-
tones that many people carry concerning these functions.
"Uptight" attitudes can be transmitted to the child and
show up later as posture/structure problems. Contracted
buttocks and anus, retracted genitals, and bed wetting
might surface as a response to the suppression of natural
feelings. When these same children grow to adulthood they
are often the ones with hemorrhoids, prostrate and uterine
problems.

It seems that childhood is a time when the basic aspects
of character are formed. In this context "character" includes the ability to respond emotionally and physically to
environmental input. We develop strategies for protecting
ourselves and for getting what we want. We learn to defend
ourselves against the expectations and criticisms of our
parents and peers. If we fail to respond in an accepted
fashion, they may react with anger and derision, further
reinforcing our defenses. If these patterns are continued,
they become stuck, or set, and will continue, in varying
degrees, into adulthood. If parental discipline becomes a
form of abuse, a whole set of body and character holding
patterns will evolve as defense responses. Steven came
from a strongly traditional mid-Western family that believed in spanking as a disciplinary measure. Steven's father
used to spank him with a leather strap whenever he felt he
was out of line. In anticipation of the discomfort, Steven
would tighten his buttocks and grip with his legs. Repetition set this contracted pattern deeply into his structure.
When Steven came to be Rolfed, I remarked about the
tight set of his legs and buttocks. He replied "I've always
had tight, really skinny legs." (Figures 5A-B) It wasn't
until his later sessions that Steven realized the connection
between the set of his legs and buttocks and the numerous
spankings he'd received until he was seventeen years old.
Even in adulthood Steven's body was still "on hold" in
anticipation of his next "spanking" (verbal or physical).

FIGURE 5A

FIGURE 5B
The body that has more of an anal retraction or holding pattern carries its "tail" (coccyx), between the legs a little like a frightened animal.

Out of love or fear, it is common for children to imitate their parents. If the father's or mother's body is stiff or awkward, this style of movement may be taken on by the child. When we look at people from the same family it is easy to see strong patterns of imitation occurring. One boy took on the stance, set of chest, shoulders, and head carriage of his father. They both breathed very shallowly and habitually tightened their buttocks. The father was amazed when I showed him photographs of him and his son.

The way in which children are programmed to become what their parents consider "adult" can drastically shape their bodies. Children are sensitive and emotional. A simple command such as "big boys don't cry" is guaranteed to kill emotional spontaneity, and dramatically tighten chest muscles and ribcage which, if continually suppressed, may surface later as hay fever, asthma, or other chronic respiratory difficulties. I am saying that emotional patterns are expressed through the structure and to repress them requires contraction in the body. To keep from crying you flex abdominal muscles, draw in the solar plexus, and stop the flow of breathing movement in the ribs. All of these reactions serve to lock in the waves of emotion. Suppressing the natural movement of the breath keeps the emotion from flowing up the chest through the throat to the jaws and lips. These flexion patterns and their attendant symptoms (asthma, etc.) have replaced the natural expression of weeping and will appear when strong emotions activate the patterns of suppression. In other words, instead of crying or expressing anger when such a response should be forthcoming, a person may get "their symptom" (allergies, asthma, stomach trouble, etc.) instead.

Children's bodies can be further shaped by parental and peer influences which encourage them to play with "appropriate" toys and to play the "right" games for their sex. Generally, boys play with cars, war toys and sports, while girls are encouraged to play with dolls or to "play house." Boys use large motor skills and use their whole bodies in play, while girls are taught to use fine motor skills and to use their bodies less vigorously. These influences shape body image and posture as well as patterns of emotional responsiveness.

When children enter school, they begin a rigorous program of socialization. In our culture we have low priority for body understanding. Freedom of expression and body exploration are largely unsupported. Anti-body, anti-feeling training is pervasive in the education system. We push children away from relying on feelings and intuition by imposing a system which rewards intellect, logic, and linear thinking. They are expected to sit still for hours on end. This focus denies the spontaneous appreciation of an inner life. Signs of body distress are belittled as "growing pains" as we continuously encourage a child to "tell us what's on your mind." Because no one recognizes or teaches normal body movement, the way a child sits, stands and walks continues to reinforce already existing imbalances in the body. The most we communicate to a child in this area are generalized directions to "sit or stand up straight." The problem is that we don't define "straight" for the child, therefore he becomes rigid in an effort to hold what he considers an upright stance.

A fall from the playground slide may injure the tailbone (coccyx) adding a physical insult to the holding pattern already in place in the buttocks from insensitive toilet training. Falls from early attempts at bicycle riding may displace ribs or shoulder. The body records these incidents in the flesh and character, making us who and how we are as adults. The point is not to demonstrate how dangerous growing up is, but to show how the accumulation of everyday experiences can be patterned into your body. Unless people are released from the structural effects of these traumas their lives will be limited by them.

A woman in her early 30s came for Rolfing with many complaints about problems in her pelvic region. She experienced frequent pain around her tail and "sitz" bones and lower abdominal cramping. She had irregular periods and had never had a satisfying sexual experience. As a young girl, she had taken a bad fall right on her tailbone while ice skating on a neighborhood pond.

"I remember falling and landing squarely on my tailbone — nothing else broke my momentum. The wind was knocked out of me and I was dizzy, but I soon recovered and continued to skate the rest of the afternoon. Two days later I could hardly walk and spent five days in bed or soaking in a hot tub. The doctor said it had cracked but would heal on its own and I'd be fine. Now I'm not so sure."

This significant structural trauma had not been totally released from her body even though it took many years for symptoms to appear.

As we move toward adolescence, we reject parental influence and are guided by peer pressure. Wearing the "right" clothes, being in the "right" groups, a rising sexual awareness and conflicting family and social mores can all cause further holding in the body. Adolescents quite often change their posture in an effort to either hide or flaunt the significant physical and glandular changes occurring in their bodies. If a woman begins to develop large breasts at a very young age, she may become extremely self-conscious and attempt to hide her development by slouching, causing her chest to cave in and her shoulders to round forward. By the mid twenties, her body is stuck in this old protective pattern, causing her to still be reserved and self-conscious, with great difficulty expressing her feelings "up front."

A 40 year old client had just the opposite condition and found herself overcompensating for her very small breasts by thrusting her chest forward and up. This jammed her middle back and spine forward while pinning her neck and shoulder blades in a "locked back" position. She had a tendency to over-do, to force herself and her ideas on others less aggressive than she. Halfway through her fifth session of Rolfing she remarked

"You know, I'm beginning to realize that I don't need to present such a pushy front to force people to accept me. I guess under it all I've been afraid to find out what I really feel in here (pointing to her chest)."

Like the previous examples, so many of us in adulthood are dramatizing emotional patterns with the body which were formed during adolescence — we are in a structural time warp.

Adding to a teenager's problems are long school hours (mostly sitting), reinforcement for "good" behavior and punishment for those who are unable or unwilling to conform to the system. Many end up as robots or rebels. The middle ground is difficult to live in.

Traditionally for males, and more recently for females, involvement in athletics is stressed as an outlet for pressures and as a place to show achievement. (Figure 5C) It is also loaded with expectations and potential disappointment. The role model here is strength, endurance, power, aggression, "sportsmanship," and winning. This supports a "macho" image with a focus on outer (extrinsic) musculature and endurance (cardiovascular capacity). The sheer joy of play and body movement is not encouraged. This sets up a pass/fail program for our youth, alienating the less gifted from themselves and their peers and severely limiting their ability to simply enjoy the game. The end result is that performance is rewarded and the process of a meaningful experience of the body is largely ignored. Athletic develop-

FIGURE 5C

ment is carried on with little or no recognition of the unique patterns in each person's body. Weight training is often encouraged at a very early age. We stress strength and achievement over balance and grace. When the musculature is developed in the training process without an eye for what is already in place, then the existing imbalances are driven deeper into the structure. Someone who already holds their chest high and breast bone pushed forward will probably have their shoulders pulled way back. This will deepen the curve in their upper back and force their spine too far forward at the shoulder blades. Doing bench presses or military presses with weights will only lock this pattern in deeper and force other areas of the body to compensate for this imbalance. Imbalances surface later as places where chronic injuries occur. It is not uncommon for the same ankle to be injured many times, or the same knee to be strained over and over. An imbalanced movement pattern will place continuous strain on the joints involved and increase the likelihood of injury. If training programs paid more attention to balanced development, they could avoid reinforcing these patterns of strain.

Consider the impact that the athletic model can have on body function and self image. The chest muscles can be pumped up so much that they will compress the upper rib structure and interfere with free breathing. Over-developed shoulder and back muscles can force the neck too far forward and restrict its normal range of motion. This causes any arm movement to push stress into the neck and compress blood vessels, decreasing circulation to the head. The one hundred sit-ups a day that "coach" prescribes will compress the rib cage by tightening the upper attachments of the belly muscles (rectus abdominus) on the front of the rib cage. Sit-ups will also reinforce unconscious sucking in of the belly and impede spontaneous flow of emotion through the solar plexus. Part of the cultural stereotype regarding males' hips is that side-to-side movement is effeminate and to be avoided. Most teenage boys interpret this as a restriction on any pelvic movement at all, and end up inhibiting both graceful movement and sexual responsiveness. Valuing body types with external muscular development begins very early in sports programs and physical education classes. I am not against physical fitness development for children. I am building a case for much greater scrutiny of the universal application of exercise and training techniques which have no regard for individual needs. There is talk of developing the whole body during adolescence, yet only lip service is given to this idea. Most gym classes stress multiple repetitions of exercise for every student, with emphasis on quantity rather than quality. There is little focus on internal lengthening (commonly called stretching) to create flexibility and fluidity of movement. Students are conditioned to think that movement involves effort and strain — to "tough it out." Children who have structural difficulties and can't follow the program are labeled "uncoordinated" or "under developed" and are left to fend for themselves, while the "good" athletes are encouraged. Children should be taught to move with awareness, not out of habit, so that movement becomes nourishing and exciting, increasing ease and flow of energy in the body.[6]

If there was more awareness of the fact that subtle imbalances or holding patterns can seriously undermine a person's ability or incentive, this would result in programs that emphasize balanced development, movement exploration, and concern for individual differences. These programs would create a much higher percentage of success in athletics for all children and a more careful directing of children into areas where their abilities would shine.

Advertising exerts a powerful effect on an adolescent's self-image. Ads are carefully developed by experts in psychological motivation. Their interest is not in the well-being of the consumer, but in creating a market for products. The advertising image is so powerful, and so subtle, that we often don't realize the extent to which it shapes us and our culture. Industry creates a whole network of false needs which perpetuate sex role stereotyping. The call to "have the best" or "look the best" often overshadows the more important need to feel and function well. "Having" is valued over "being." While advertising for children fo-

6.   See the chapters Body-Work and Body Play for a more complete discussion of movement awareness. Also consult Appendix B.

cuses on food and toys, the messages directed toward adolescents and adults are primarily concerned with the creation of an image. A teenager looking through a fashion magazine will find that every woman is slinky, wears high heels and the current look. If she doesn't match that picture she isn't "with it." If she doesn't use deodorant she can't possibly get a date. If she has bad breath no one will love her. The ads don't mention that bad breath may be a sign of a digestive disorder, or that "bad breath" may be your "up-tightness" coming through. The thrust of the advertising is toward camouflage — the real you is not acceptable.

Clothes can be used as camouflage too, keeping us from ourselves as well as others. In the same way that young athletes put a muscular casing around themselves, styles of clothing can be used as a cover and can greatly affect our sense of self. Advertisements tend to objectify and classify us into specific categories — the "sexy look," the "macho look," the "young executive," and the "career woman," the "housewife," and the "casual look," etc. There is no regard for the potentially alienating and limiting effect on body and self that adherence to these images can create. These stereotypes make it easier to assign responsibility for our condition to something outside ourselves, precisely because we are taking our direction from these externally prescribed roles. These efforts to build an image are statements about our vulnerability. All this posturing provides a layer of protection which keeps us from ourselves and from others. The body is not an image, it is our reality. It is our inner being that is in need of nourishment and animation. To be balanced we must re-establish contact with our inner self and integrate that awareness with our body, especially during these most vulnerable stages of childhood/adolescence.

At this stage of development many children (mostly girls) are discovered to have scoliosis, a side-to-side or spiral deviation of the spine from normal. This seems to be the only structural imbalance that schools normally screen for. Perhaps because of puberty the body is at a point where it simply cannot absorb any more strain, so the body components begin to give way under continual pressure. Traditionally, this problem is dealt with locally, either by spinal surgery, braces, or body casts, with little consideration given to the underlying causes of the curvature. Rolfing experience suggests that a difficult birth process, in which the cranium was stressed in the birth canal and deformed in a subtle way (possibly by medical intervention with forceps) is one method which can contribute to spinal curvature in later development. It is interesting to note that many of the young people who have developed juvenile scoliosis also had early orthopedic intervention (leg casts, braces, splints, corrective shoes, or surgery) to correct turned-in or turned-out feet. Many also had early and extensive orthodontia.[7] It is possible that these early leg patterns were expressions of (or resulted from) structural strain and imbalance in the pelvis and spine. The attempts to correct the pattern by trying to force the feet into alignment eliminates an avenue of release for the primary, sometimes deeper lying structural distress. Or perhaps the correction (orthopedic intervention) imposed upon the leg pattern resulted in the structural stress moving up the body, causing spinal rotations to be created to absorb the forced changes. Not enough is known as yet to know for sure how some of these juvenile scoliosis problems occur, but it may suggest that a more comprehensive assessment of structural imbalance and resultant compensations may need to be considered. (Figure 6 — Scoliosis)

7.   New information is also suggesting that sleep position patterns may have impact upon posture and spinal curves. See Hal Huggins, *Why Raise Ugly Kids?* in the bibliography.

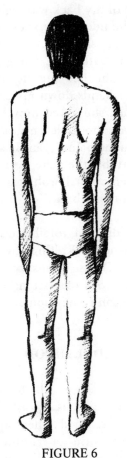

FIGURE 6
The pressures from this type of spinal pattern cause adjustments thoughout the entire body.

Denise is an intelligent woman in her early thirties. She has two children and recently returned to school to study law. She came to get Rolfed because she has scoliosis and is constantly in pain.

"For a long time I remember sitting in the bath and

feeling that one side of my back was higher than the other. I could make one shoulder blade stick out more than the other. One night I was slumped over in the tub and my mother came into the bathroom. She glanced at me in the mirror and gasped. She had me sit straight and slump slowly as she ran her hands down my spine. With a horrified look on her face she asked how long my back had been that way — I was about eleven years old. When I was eighteen the continuous pain began. It started out only as a physical pain, but by the time I turned twenty-five I realized that all my emotional problems and pressures were intensifying the pain in my back."

Although her spine did not totally straighten during the initial ten-hour sequence of Rolfing, she did get relief from the painful spasms. Denise plans on returning in nine months for another series of sessions to see if more unwinding of her curve can come about.

ADULTHOOD

In our culture, the age at which the "line" between adolescence and adulthood is crossed varies greatly. In general, adulthood is reached when we assume worldly responsibility of one form or another. In "primitive" cultures, and those with strong religious structure, we find definite rites of passage. These are characterized by the community of elders collectively affirming that the young person is now an adult. This usually happens around age thirteen and is accompanied by the assumption of specific duties in the community after certain rituals have been completed. Each individual is moved clearly and absolutely into adulthood. He or she can feel, deeply within, that "I am a man, or woman" and that their childhood is completed.

In our culture, the "passage" is, in most cases, quite vague. There is a large grey area to be crossed, with no clear affirmation from the community telling you that you have arrived. It is not unusual to see people well into their thirties still acting like teenagers.[8] There is an idealization of youth, an elevated image about how we must stay young. This ambiguous state bordering on adulthood is a difficult one. Lack of clarity on how to "graduate" is confusing to those caught in this state.

The arrival at a job, marriage, the military or whatever the assumption of responsibility entails, is also accompanied by the addition of more stress as "old" patterns of behavior conflict with new demands. Some of the stress-responses that were established earlier in life may now go a step further and emerge as "symptoms." These symptoms are assigned various labels — such as "nervous tension headaches," "insomnia," "constipation," or "low energy." Eventually they may emerge as chronic pain and lead into diagnosed illness or disease. Colitis, bursitis, arthritis, sciatica and ulcers are often outward signs of a lifetime of accumulated stress, poor diet and lack of exercise all taking their toll upon the structural balance of the body.[9]

Steven the client who was spanked a lot as a child, is a good example of someone whose problems as an adult are a result of many years of accumulated tension. At the time of his Rolfing he was also being treated by his family doctor for varicose veins and high blood pressure. Because his legs were so tight, the connective tissues thickened and his circulation was hampered, raising the pressure necessary

8.   Separating from strong parental influence is often very difficult. In my practice I find many adults whose bodies and minds seem to "belong" to their parents. It is as if such people are waiting for some special permission to come alive.
9.   Because so many jobs are of a sedentary nature, inactivity is now a primary contributor to the so-called hypokinetic conditions. The most common are illnesses involving the heart and blood vessels, emotional disorders and muscular deficiencies.

to move fluid through his legs. Steven's condition may be the result of holding his legs tightly in anticipation of the next "spanking" — either verbal or physical. This is something that we worked on throughout his Rolfing sessions — the constant state of over-readiness in his body and his unwillingness to let down his guard. As the tension in his body was released, Steven felt less defensive and more at home in his body, and almost simultaneously his blood pressure dropped to acceptable levels.

When Simon came to get Rolfed he had a long history of medical problems, including two colon surgeries. His lifestyle offers some clues as to why these problems may have occurred. He has recently turned forty. Simon's job is a high stress one, as he oversees the work of twenty employees and is responsible to the front office if production is down or orders get fouled up. He drinks a lot after work and regularly eats in restaurants, consuming a diet of rich and highly processed foods. He doesn't get much exercise any more, except "sit-ups and push-ups every day to keep the old front in shape." The Rolfing work began to increase Simon's level of awareness. He realized that his unhealthy lifestyle was causing the majority of his medical and structural problems. As he began to experience new balance in his body, he felt hopeful that he could change other areas of his life into a more healthy pattern.

FULL MATURITY

In the "last" phase of life, we find that expectations about aging, coupled with physical history, go a long way toward determining how well people are doing. If the body has been abused and has accumulated trauma and tension, then a gradual slowing of the movement of fluids in the tissues will be felt as "old age." So often those who retire at sixty-five from an active working life rapidly lose their vitality and interest. At this point they seem to age more quickly. On the other hand, there are "elders" who stay active, engaging in sports, hobbies, self-generated employment or community service. The difference seems to be, at least in part, how the person's expectations of aging are made real. If you focus on the outward form, a lack of tone in the soft tissue, and the changes in life rhythm, then the person's identity becomes threatened. If not actually said out loud, the feeling is ". . . I am not the person I used to be." The pressures of time and the feelings of regret about not having achieved certain things become more intensified, while the inevitability of death is brought to higher awareness. After many years of imbalance and extra effort, the accumulation of trauma to the structure shows up as a loss of body form, a restriction of fluid movement, and a diminished ability to adapt mentally and physically. Such a person is losing his fight with gravity.[10]

Simply stated, aging is a progressive loss of both internal and external movement in the body. Too often I see people who are "old" in the sense that the health and age of their tissue is far beyond their chronological age. One of the factors to consider in determining the "age" of a body is the ease with which fluids move through the muscles and connective tissues and the amount of fluid in the tissues. At one pole we see bodies where the deepest tissues dry out or become dehydrated, causing a "brittle" quality in the body. At the other extreme we see structures with excessive fluid which over time deteriorates the tone of the flesh making the body puffy or soggy. Neither is healthy and each indicates different forms of imbalance in the structure and usually something about the emotional style of dealing with stress.[11]

10. See the chapter "Gravity is The Glue" for a discussion of the relationship between gravity and body structure.
11. See the Discussion in Chapter 10, "Body Work," on body types, emotional stress, and character patterns.

When an elder recognizes the changes in body form and function for what they are and maintains an active involvement in life, old age can be a time of exciting growth and exploration. In traditional cultures, the last years are a time when the greatest spiritual growth is possible, a time to live life gracefully in preparation for a dignified death. With a release from worldly duties there is a deepening of inner awareness. The elders are seen as advisors, their accumulated experience and wisdom are sought and appreciated. With the breakdown of the family in the West, these traditonal roles are being lost. It is now the responsibility of the individual to keep his life worth living, to keep growing, and to find a place where his contribution can be used. A balanced body structure makes this task much easier.

CONCLUSION

Lack of balance and movement in our physical structures prevents an integration of body, mind, and spirit. When a person is chronically "stuck" they are unable to "empty their cup," to absorb new life energy. Frequent physical and emotional pain are the outward signs of stuckness. This inhibits our instinctual life and spontaneity. We get out of touch with that inner process which allows us to distinguish the greater from the lesser truths in life. Our movement patterns, our metabolism, and our mental and emotional health become stressed and fail to function properly.

There is hope for a higher level of well-being in all stages of life. With Rolfing, the flexed and hardened tissues can be opened up, allowing fluids to move again, irrigating and vitalizing the whole body. With the recognition that balance in the flesh leads to higher levels of function in the whole person, comes the possibility of another means of developing our unique nature as individuals. To be less bound by the flesh, less locked into a single pattern of response to the world, allows the movement of one's life a wider range. As one's own balance and integration are upgraded it becomes possible to see beyond one's personal life to the life of the whole. In effect, we can then consciously move in relation to the world around us. In this state, our journey through the flesh will be a most rewarding one. The next chapters describe the specific components of a new organization for our bodies which supports a healthy journey.

3

GRAVITY IS THE GLUE

Gravity is always there; you can never escape from it. From the day that single cell is fertilized and develops, gravity is with it. The fetus in the woman's womb is under the effect of gravity; and until the undertaker gets the body and lays it away, it's under the effect of gravity.

I.P.R.

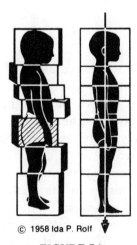

© 1958 Ida P. Rolf

FIGURE 7A

The purpose of this chapter is to outline the basic ideas that form the foundation of the Rolfing system. Three important factors will be examined which affect the human structure — gravity, the organization of the major body segments (head, chest, pelvis, legs), and the connective tissue. Rolfing is unique because it works with structure while simultaneously considering the effect of gravity on the body segments and the response of the connective tissues. Because we live in time and to a certain extent build our character as we accumulate experience, the factors of time and character interact with the physical factors of gravity, body segments, and connective tissue. By evaluating body structure, character and tissue age, a Rolfer is able to determine the current level of stress in a body, as well as predicting what future structural problems may arise if the imbalances are not removed. By considering the relationship of gravity, body segments, connective tissue and character, we can arrive at an idea of what is "normal" for how human beings should age healthfully.

GRAVITY

When Dr. Rolf was asked about the most important aspect of her system, she replied, "Gravity — if you throw out gravity you've thrown out Rolfing." Understanding the influence of gravity on human structure is essential to understanding body alignment. In Newtonian physics, gravity is considered to be a force or an attraction that develops between material substances. Gravity governs all matter in its relationship to the earth. Newton's famous apple proved that the earth and the apple are in a gravitational relationship. They are attracted to one another. The apple will always fall to the earth — its mass is less and it must yield to the greater mass of the earth. The apple will always fall straight down, because gravity operates through the center of mass of objects. The same relationship exists between a human and the earth. As the earth's mass is so much greater than our own, we must do the adapting —

not the earth. Gravity never takes a vacation; we live in gravity as a fish lives in water, its influence is continuous and pervasive. Balancing becomes easier as the body approaches a more vertical stance. As one's body begins to balance better, less energy will be required to keep it there. It takes less energy to maintain balance than to obtain it. If the body is struggling with gravity, more energy will be used in moving. Rolfers have observed that bodies working against gravity become more contracted over time and progressively lose their alignment because of the extra effort needed to remain upright. Rolfing helps people to become more conscious of gravity's ever-present influence and to work with it, not against it.

The Rolf logo illustrates an integrated relationship between man and the earth, with gravity as the glue that holds everything together.

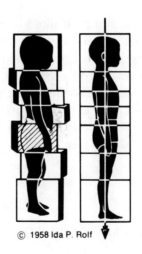

© 1958 Ida P. Rolf

FIGURE 7B

Gravity acts as responsive "glue" when the body segments are aligned and balanced on top of one another. If the segments are out of alignment, the "glue" hardens in an attempt to hold the body segments "up" against the downward pull of gravity. As the glue hardens (tissues tighten), gravity creates more stress on individual segments and pulls the body towards earth, giving it a heavy appearance and feeling. If the body is in proper alignment, it will keep the glue fluid and gravity will support and balance the segments. A balanced body allows one to feel more secure in the gravity field. By living in harmony with gravity, we can relax and stop bracing against it and begin using gravity to increase structural order and free our energy to live a fuller life. When clients come for Rolfing they often complain of feeling heavy or pulled down into their bodies. Actually, they are describing how their bodies are experiencing the influence of gravity. The following reflects one person's account of their changing relationship with gravity:

"Before I was Rolfed I felt like I weighed two hundred pounds. (Her actual weight was 120 pounds.) Everything felt like such a drag. My posture was bad. I didn't have any energy, so I chose not to do very much. After my seventh session, when my shoulders finally let go of my neck, I felt like the world had been lifted from my back. At first I laughed a lot because I felt light as a balloon. I noticed my willingness to take on new projects with a real sense of enthusiasm."

FASCIA – THE ORGAN OF SUPPORT

Another key to understanding this view of human structure is the plastic, or changeable, nature of the connective tissues. For our purposes, these tissues include tendons, ligaments, muscles, cartilage, bones, and various forms of fascia which wrap and position these other con-

nective tissues.[1] All forms of connective tissue originate
from the same kind of cells. Each type is unique by vir-
tue of its varying degree of elasticity and inorganic salt
content — i.e., bone is less elastic than tendon because it
possesses a larger salt content. Ligaments and tendons get
their unique texture from the varying amounts of fiber
they contain. These fibers align with the direction of the
forces they are subject to. For example, if in standing and
walking you bear more weight on the outside portions of
your feet and legs, the fiber will tend to build up more in
those areas. The amount of fiber determines how elastic
the tissue is — more fiber equals less elasticity. The ligaments that help maintain bones in position are heavily
fibered with very little stretch. They must be this tough to
keep joints from moving beyond their normal range. Tendons are less dense as they function as extensions and par-
titions of muscle structure. Their total fiber content is less
than ligaments; they are therefore more elastic with greater
range of stretch potential. The looser connective tissues
which wrap around abdominal organs have relatively little
fiber and are very elastic. Each of these tissue types has different levels of circulation. The denser and more fibrous
ligaments have limited circulation and would tend to heal
more slowly after an injury or surgery than would the
more elastic tissues. Because the function of these tissues is
so diverse, they have never been formally classified as a
system in themselves. Rolfing views the fascial network as
an organ which transmits and distributes movement and
gives the body internal support and external form.

Fascia resembles a totally interconnected seamless
body stocking stretching under the skin. This fascial "net"

---

1.   Apponeuroses, interosseous membranes, septa, muscular inscriptions,
retinaculae, and deep and superficial forms of fascia are distributed throughout the body according to functional need. All of these can be considered dif-
ferentiated forms of connective tissue.

not only wraps the whole body, it also winds throughout the structure from surface to deep layers. It wraps all the muscles and forms the sheaths that divide muscle groups into their functional compartments. At the deepest layer, these wrappings become continuous with the membranes (periosteum) covering the bones. The fascia around the organs is formed into webs, strings and packing material, to keep the organs supported and positioned in proper relationship to the rest of the body. (Figure 8) All body parts are wrapped in, connected by, or related through various forms of fascia. This creates an intricate web of connections which serve as a medium for the transmission

FIGURE 8

Under a microscope certain forms of fascia look like stretched cotton candy or gauze. Its total interconnectedness truly makes it the body's organ of internal support.

of impulses and responses from deep in our body to the surface. This connection is a two-way street. Our response to outside pressures runs back along fascial pathways to the depths of our structure. Reflexes from our deepest organs move to the surface along these same channels.

Let's examine some of the special qualities of connective tissue. The basic unit of connective tissue is collagen, a coiled protein molecule capable of conducting impulses.[2] Collagens have the unique property of being mutable. They are a bit like water, which changes from solid ice to crystalline snow, to fluid and finally to vapor in response to environmental influences. Collagen can be very "gel" (dense) when little fluid is moving through it, or it can change to a "sol" or fluid state when it receives adequate energy in the form of heat or pressure. It is this range of resilience that makes the fascia responsive to changes in body form and balance. If the body is knocked out of alignment in an accident, pathways of movement shift and fiber is deposited, adding support to the new arrangement. A similar response occurs when the body adjusts to support habitual patterns of movement, posture and attitude. The mutable property of collagen that allows the body to alter its form can be used positively. The Rolfing process realigns the body and lengthens chronically shortened areas by manipulating and changing the fascia. Fiber and gristle are the raw materials from which length is created in a body. Hardened tissues are metabolized, fluid flow is increased, toxins are discharged and tissue is retoned as gravity's pressure is eased. When the segments realign themselves the whole body/person enters a new and more balanced relationship with gravity. Rolfing manipulation changes the consistency of the tissue and redistributes the

2.   The Connective Tissue and Myofascial Systems, James L. Oschman, Ph.D., The Marine Biological Lab, Woods Hole, Mass. 02543, p. 16. Also The Aspen Research Institute, 1430 LeRoy Ave., Berkeley Calif., 94708, 1981.

fiber, which results in improved support and alignment in the entire structure.[3]

SEGMENTATION

The body can be viewed as being comprised of a number of weight blocks, or segments. These segments are the head, trunk (thorax), pelvis, legs and arms. Each segment is hinged to its neighbor through the joints and connective tissues which bind them. This hinging action can be seen in the nodding of the head on the neck, bending movements at the waist, swinging of the knee in walking and in the movements at the elbow, wrist and ankle. Proper hinge function is a sign of order in the relationship of bones and soft tissues. This order allows a fluid movement style. Because of the amazingly plastic quality of connective tissue, body segments can change their alignment rather rapidly. If the centers of gravity of each segment are aligned with one another, gravity is better able to support each segment as well as the whole body. If the segments become unbalanced, we find that gravity starts to "drag" on them and over time will make the problem worse. (Figure 9A-B) Keep in mind that the main response of the body to continual imbalance is to tighten muscles and add fiber in the areas of stress. In the short term, this will be effective in helping the body to maintain its alignment. However, over time, fiber accumulates, tissues thicken and the body loses its elasticity and mobility. As the stresses continue over time, the body loses vitality and the ability to cope with the stress of life.

3.   For a more complete description of the processes of Rolfing manipulation, see *Rolfing: The Integration of Human Structures*, Ida P. Rolf, Dennis Landman, 1977, hardcover, or a softcover version reprinted by Harper and Row Publishers.

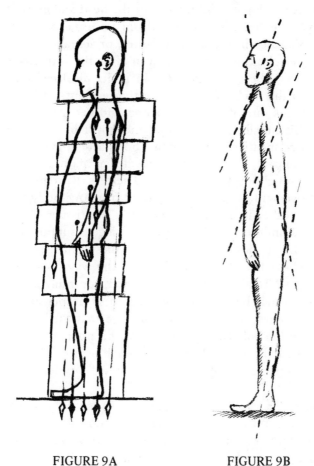

FIGURE 9A   FIGURE 9B
A misaligned body experiences gravity as one continuous "drag."

To illustrate the interplay of gravity, segmentation and connective tissue, let's consider a typical whiplash accident. The mechanics of a whiplash involve a sudden acceleration of the body. The neck receives most of the strain as the head segment lags behind and then returns, like a cracking whip. The muscles of the neck may have some torn fibers, making it painful to carry the head and move it normally. The head is displaced from its usual position, due to imbalance in the injured tissues, or actual displacement of vertebrae in the neck. Even after the torn tissue has "healed," the head may remain in its displaced relationship to the neck. We then have the segments of head, neck and ribs out of relation to one another. As gravity acts on this imbalance over time, there will be a further change in connective tissue. When a body attempts to integrate the impact of an injury, it creates a "path of adaptation" throughout the structure. There is a progressive loss of movement as the stress is passed from one body segment to another in a "domino effect." The tissues of the upper back and neck will begin thickening to support the disorder. In an attempt to integrate these changes, the whole body will make subtle shifts all the way down the legs and feet. The torn tissues will mend, returning somewhat to normal, but usually the pattern of deeper imbalance will remain. We are usually unaware that the body is still held in the imbalanced pattern. At this point the body has absorbed the original injury as much as possible, but it may be setting up the body for a "new" problem later on.

Taken as a whole, these components (gravity, segmentation and connective tissue) are the framework for a model of development for human structure. From this we can arrive at a definition for normal which is based on simple and clearly defined principles of how the body works best. This model allows for human variability and uniqueness. These observations on human structure can be applied to all people, whether short or tall, big boned or small boned, male or female. We all have bodies and they all must operate in the field of gravity. The more balanced and aligned our bodies are, the more we are free to meet our potential and to continue with our development. Along with a definition of normal, this vision is unique because it focuses upon structure, putting together the elements of body/mind in an efficient energy system that supports the body's inherent drive toward balance. The alleviation of symptoms is not the only sign of true health. A truly healthy person is balanced in body, mind and spirit and therefore is efficient, vital, and adaptable.

"Our job is the situation that gravity can mend."
Ida P. Rolf, Ph.D.

4

SKELETON
The Bony Architecture

In a human body, support is not something solid. Support is relationship. Support is balance of elements that aren't solid at all, elements that are incapable of withstanding the weight that presses down on them except as they are balanced.

I.P.R.

In a living body, bone is quite different from the prepared skeletons seen in anatomy labs. A mounted skeleton gives one the impression that it is hard, brittle, and somehow separate from the flesh. Nothing could be further from the truth. Living healthy bone is rich in blood supply and quite flexible. The skeleton is made up of the same basic structural elements as the other connective tissues, except for a greater content of inorganic salts, which provide the bones with needed strength and rigidity. Recent studies with radioactive isotopes show that bony material is replaced in as little as seven months.[1] This indicates that bone is vitally alive and metabolically active.[2] Bones are not merely the attachment points for muscles, but are embedded in the flesh, wrapped in elastic connective tissue membranes called the periosteum. Muscles and ligaments

---

1. E.W. Russell, *Design For Destiny*, Neville Spearman Ltd., London, 1971.
2. See Robert Becker and Andrew Morino, *Electro-Magnetism and Life*, SUNY Press, Albany, N.Y. 1982 for new information on the aliveness of bone and its regenerative capacities.

find their attachments to the bones by rooting through the perisoteum, much as a tree is rooted in and becomes part of the earth in which it grows.

This model of the body emphasizes the interplay between the skeleton and the web of soft tissue in which it is embedded. If you look at a drawing of the skeleton you may get the impression that the bones hold up the body and that the muscles hang from the bones. The Rolfing view suggests nearly the opposite: that the bone, fluid in the joint capsule, and the ligaments and muscles combine to provide the means by which the weight of the body is managed. By considering the relationship of bones to soft tissue we see that the bones act primarily as struts or spacers, keeping the soft tissues spread and positioned. Normally, the relationship between bone and soft tissue is unstressed and the soft tissue is able to share in the support of the body's weight. The bones only receive compressional forces under unusual strain or if a joint becomes misaligned. Weight going through the body is also shared by the fluid capsules between the joints and the binding ligaments around the joints. These lubricate the joints and act like the shock absorbers in a car. True lightness of movement comes into a body as weight management is shifted off the skeleton and onto the soft tissues in a reciprocal relationship. Considering the bony framework in this way gives us a somewhat different view of how structural problems occur.

It is only when the spine is asked to act as a columnar weight-bearing unit that the collection of structural failures we call "back trouble" begins to show up. The disc functions as a spacer and shock absorber, cushioning unusual forces that "leak" into the spine from various movements. Improper alignment of vertebrae disrupts the balance of the ligaments, forcing the discs to act full time in a weight-bearing capacity. If there is a failure in the span and tone of the soft tissue around the joint, then the disc material may protrude from between the vertebral bodies, pressing on nearby nerves and creating debilitating pain. (Figure 10) It should be emphasized that I am talking about degenerative processes rather than injuries, as an injury can be local and specific to a given spinal joint. The degeneration of spinal order is a long term affair, involving

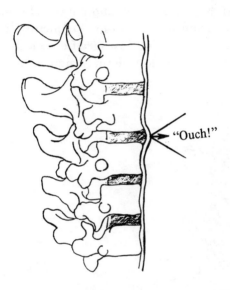

"Ouch!"

FIGURE 10
Even slight misalignment of a vertebrae can compress and displace a disc.

an accumulation of stresses from the entire body. Clear evidence for the soft tissues' role as a suspensory mechanism can be seen in the structure of the spinal vertebrae. If the spine was designed to bear weight as a column then it would seem that the bodies of the vertebrae would be more dense. However, the greater density in the vertebrae is all in the spinous and transverse processes where the ligaments and muscles attach. These portions of the vertebrae do not bear directly on one another, so weight cannot be transmitted as in a columnar structure. (Figure 11) On the basis of this structural evidence, the notion (so prevalent in the sciences of orthopedics, traditional anatomy and chiropractic) that the bony vertebrae are the primary weight-bearing mechanism must be re-examined and reevaluated.[3]

I have many clients who come to be Rolfed because they are suffering from pain and continual discomfort in their low back and spinal regions. Frequently these conditions do not arise out of any specific accident or injury, but are the result of long term structural imbalance. A

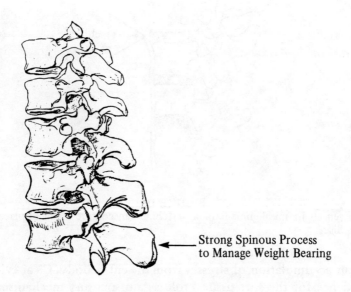

Strong Spinous Process
to Manage Weight Bearing

FIGURE 11
Body weight is managed cooperatively by bone and soft tissues.

3.   David L. Robbie, M.D., "Tensional Forces in The Human Body," Orthopaedic Review, Vol. VI, No. 11, Nov., 1977.

spine that has been doing more than its fair share of weight bearing will in time talk back with pain, discomfort and some degeneration. Structural realignment from Rolfing can help reverse this progressive destruction and re-balance the weight-bearing load between the soft tissues and the skeleton, creating appropriate lift in the spine and allowing the person more comfort in their lives.

Now that we have examined some ideas about skeletal structure we can discuss some important functions in this region of the body. In the early part of this century a student of Osteopathy, Will Sutherland, had a flash of inspiration while studying the parts of a human skull. He observed that the sutures, or joints, of the skull were designed to overlap ". . . beveled like the gills of a fish, for articulation."[4] (Figures 12A-B) Traditional medical thinking believes that the 29 bones of the cranium gradually

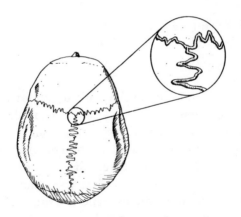

FIGURE 12A
Close-up of Beveled Cranial Sutures

4.   Sutherland, W. G. *The Cranial Bowl*, Mankato, MN: W. G. Sutherland, 1939.

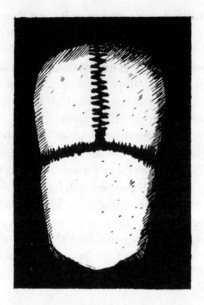

FIGURE 12B
In a healthy body the cranial bones should not be fused into a solid
unit.

fuse to form a solid, immovable unit by about the age of
twenty-five. In light of this you can imagine that Sutherland's ideas of a moving and responsive cranium were not
well received by the medical establishment. He persisted in
his research and practice, however, and went on to demonstrate a limited and specifically patterned movement that
includes the cranium, the sacrum, and the spine. This movement is concerned with pressure changes in the flow of the
cerebro-spinal[5] fluid, which moves up and down the spine
like an elevator, and the pulsation of the membrane
(known as the dura mater) that wraps the brain and spinal

5.   A water envelope that bathes and nourishes the brain and spinal cord and
cushions them from shock.

cord in response to these pressure changes.[6,7] These ideas furthered the development of cranial osteopathy, a manipulation practice designed to normalize the pulsation in the dura mater of the brain, spine and sacrum into a rhythmic pattern. As with any inspired work, these discoveries have spread to take root in other minds and become embodied in other systems. Dr. Rolf recognized that this rhythmic fluid movement showed that the spine was functioning normally. She realized that if the bony spinal column was acting as a primary weight-bearing member, the wave of movement transmitted through the dura would be interfered with at the levels of structural compression. The existence of a well-balanced cranio-sacral "pulse" indicates that the spine is largely free from bearing more than its share of body weight. This is another landmark that Rolfers have begun to use in their evaluation of a balanced body.

In the discussion of the dura mater and the cranium, spine and sacrum we have been describing physical structures in the body. There is also a functional center which we call the core. The core is the gravitational center of the body, expressing the way a person organizes his body in space in relation to gravity. The core is not a fixed place; it shifts around, compresses or expands, depending on the position or even the mood of the person. To a Rolfer's eye the core function is the hallmark of a well-organized structure. The extent to which this core function can lengthen within the body both at rest and during movement

---

6.   Sutherland referred to this membrane as the reciprocal tension membrane and postulated that the wave of movement that he detected in the bones of the head, spine, and sacrum was the outward and visible sign of the internal contraction and release of the dura. He saw that as a separate and primary pulse, unrelated to blood flow or respiration.
7.   An excellent account of the cranio-sacral system can be found in *Craniosacral Therapy*, John Upledger and Jon Vredevoogd, Eastland Press, Chicago, 1983.

determines the degree of balance and integration possible for that structure. We call the mass of the body around this core the sleeve. The sleeve is also a function, not a physical structure. On a "good" day when the step is light and the spine long, the core will be seen as extended and moving freely within the sleeve. If you visualize the movement of a periscope, you will get an image of how the core moves within the sleeve. Illness, injury or fatigue with a resultant heaviness of gait and loss of vitality would cause the core to be shortened and bound into the sleeve. The core/sleeve is another metaphor which describes how the weight of the body moves around its gravitational center. A well-functioning relationship between the core and sleeve suggests that the body is well-organized in relation to the line of gravity's influence upon it. In some bodies there is little or no separation between core and sleeve. At first glance, you might think that a heavyset person would have their core bound into the sleeve. This is not always true, as someone who is quite overweight may have a functional core, giving them a lightness of movement, while a very thin and tight person may have their core completely bound in their sleeve. The relationship of core and sleeve can be different in the upper and lower halves of the body. It is common for Rolfers to see clients who have their core free from their sleeve at the pelvis, for example, and restricted in the neck and shoulder region. Rolfers use the core/sleeve references as grid patterns or coordinates with actual structural landmarks that help to organize what they are seeing when observing human structures. This diagnostic tool gives excellent information about the level of balanced function in the body.

One quality of a balanced body is the separation of the core from the sleeve throughout. This can be seen as a "line" that represents the center of the body's weight extending and moving (like a periscope) freely within the structure. A body with this in place has a quality of movement which is light and fluid. This quality is more evident as the skeleton comes into alignment, and the muscular flexors and extensors[8]   which move the bones are in a more balanced relationship, and the joints transmit weight more effectively and function as true hinges. A functioning core/sleeve is easily seen in the graceful movement of wild animals. We often reference animal movement when describing aesthetically pleasing human movement — "graceful as a gazelle." I feel that movement which represents core/sleeve separation is more often observable in wild animals because they are spontaneous and not hampered by self-consciousness and character. This functional quality is also quite obtainable for humans when their bodies achieve structural balance.

8.   See page 197.

5

LEGS AND FEET
From The Ground Up

If a man weren't a standing, two-footed animal, he would have fewer problems. But since he is standing, he is walking as best as he can. He's been doing this since he was a kid — climbing up the side of his play-pen and somehow getting his legs under him. Possibly he got his legs under him very badly, but he wasn't paying any attention to that. He had one goal: he wanted to be like big brother, and big brother was able to walk.

I.P.R.

"Stand up straight." "Stand on your own two feet." "Keep on your toes." "Walk the straight and narrow." These expressions describe particular ways that we use our legs and feet. Quite often these "sayings" find literal expression in the body. It is not surprising to find people with rigid feet, inflexible ankles, or shortened and bunched leg muscles trying to support a rather uneasy "self" in the body above. The second session of Rolfing (in the basic series of 10) often focuses on the structure of the legs and feet. Most people's feet are bound tightly and overworked in certain areas and under-used in others. Many people don't feel the ground through their feet. It is as if they walk around on stilts and are not connected to how or what they feel, or to the contour of the surface that they are traveling on.

Whatever their form, it is the job of the legs to do

everything possible to keep us upright and moving. In addition to the obvious functions of support and mobility they
also serve as the "second heart." Rhythmic contractions
pump blood from the heart, but it is muscular activity in
the legs that plays a major role in the return of fluids
against gravity. Rigid musculature and thickened connective tissue increase the blood pressure needed by the heart
to return blood through the veins and lymphatic vessels.
Rolfing will release the thickened connective tissue and
give it proper tone and alignment, enabling the legs and
feet to freely support and transport. This will often result
in a decrease of blood pressure.

Gary was the youngest of five children and, as he recalls, spent a lot of time defending himself against the bul-
lying and ridicule of his older brothers. Gary's legs are extremely rigid and tightly compressed. (Figure 13) They are
very white and appear unalive, ready to crumble and top-
ple over if he is verbally assaulted one more time. His arches
are drawn up like a hand retracted in spasm. Gary is outwardly aggressive and seems quite confident. To a Rolfer,
however, his legs tell a different story. They suggest a highly controlled approach to life, as if Gary is always bracing
himself. His aggressive front is more likely a cover-up for a
very inadequate sense of self. His body has flexed one time
too many in response to a childhood filled with continual
harassment and an adulthood spent protecting a sensitive
inside. Gary recalls aspects of his childhood:

"To me, the sad part is that I honestly feel that my
brothers loved me, but I don't think they knew how to
show it. Things were always so competitive. There wasn't
much room to let down your guard and just 'be' together.
Sometimes my legs will buckle under me for no apparent
reason — even when I'm just standing and talking to someone. Locking my knees helps me to feel more secure in my
legs, but now after seeing my pictures I can see how that

makes my pelvis tilt forward."

FIGURE 13
The legs are often used to "prop up" an inadequate sense of self or to "brace" against impending assault.

It took several sessions working almost exclusively on Gary's legs before they began to soften and catch up with the maturity of the rest of his body.

If we examine the structure of the legs and feet, some fascinating aspects about their design become apparent. We see that the feet are small in relation to the amount of body mass they support. The feet literally bear the end result of all the stresses, strains, and traumas that the rest of the body has experienced; they are the structural "dump" of the body. If some part of the body is moved off center through an accident or strain, the legs and feet will receive an uneven distribution of weight. In the case of an injury that heals quickly this is of little consequence, but if the body fails to return to its former balance the legs must make an adaptive change by altering their structure. The change may take the form of over-development, such as a buildup of fibrous tissue in the stressed area causing a loss of mobility and a shift in the bones of the legs and feet as the body attempts to handle an overload of "work" coming through it. While these compensations keep the body functioning, their long term, cumulative effect may become more detrimental to the health of the person than the original injury.

One client had injured his knee by turning too sharply while playing racquetball. He injured the same knee three times over a nine-month period and didn't come to get Rolfed until he began to experience a "funny pain" in his other knee. This cross-over of pain is very common, although where the compensation will "surface" is not always predictable. I have seen people complaining of low back pain that started up following an ankle sprain, and cases in which a person's back became chronically sore as they struggled to re-balance after a leg injury. Rolfing works to balance the whole body; the compensating area (the "other" knee or neck or back) will be manipulated and aligned along with the places in the body which experience direct stress and trauma.

The foot is made up of twenty-six bones, knit together by strong ligaments (117) and muscles (19). These bones are arranged in a complex of three arches, two running the length of the foot and one across the width, just in front of the ankle. These arches must be in proper position, each bearing its share of the load from above, to insure adequate support, balance and responsiveness in the foot. (Figure 14) The whole area below the knee should have been named the "foot" to more accurately reflect how this re-

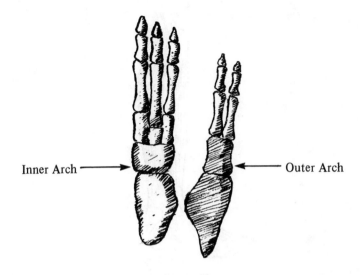

Inner Arch ──────▶   ◀────── Outer Arch

FIGURE 14

gion operates. From the drawing (Figure 15) you can see that all of the muscles in the lower leg cross the ankle joint and insert in the various bones of the foot. These structures are, in fact, part of the foot. It is our language that leads us to conceive of these as separate units, i.e. foot, lower leg. The body knows no such division. The top bone of the foot (talus) is slotted between the two bones of the lower leg in an arrangement that resembles a hinge. The shin bone (Figures 16A-B) (tibia) meets the single bone of the upper leg (femur) at the knee. The fibula is unique in that it has no socket or groove to absolutely position it in its attachment to the knee. It is only held in place by ligaments and the muscular bindings around it. This highly mobile bone adapts to changes in balance from above. It can also be displaced in an ankle sprain and may be the component that does not return to normal as the ankle heals. This is frequently the condition that sets up repeated sprains.

FIGURE 15
The lower leg muscles significantly influence the form and position of the bones of the foot.

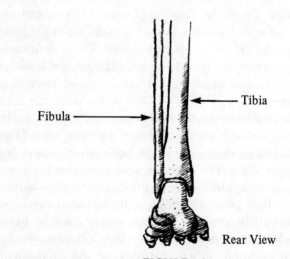

Tibia

Fibula

Rear View

FIGURE 16A
The foot (ankle) hinge is created by its relationship to the two lower leg bones.

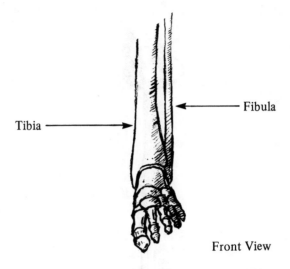

Tibia

Fibula

Front View

FIGURE 16B

The small muscles within the foot are responsible for its local movement, while the tone and order of the musculature of the lower leg helps to keep the arch from becoming too high or too flat.

Continuing in the exploration of leg structure we come to the femur again. At its top is a ball which meets with a socket in the pelvis. While this joint has a wide range of possible movements, it primarily functions as a hinge in its relationship to the knee while walking or running. The quality of the hinging action at the joints can be seen as a function of the balance of tone in soft tissues around the joints. (Figure 17) Misalignment of the lower leg in relation to the upper leg can be viewed as an imbalance of stresses between the soft tissues that cross the joints. Lack of alignment is caused by problems in the soft tissues but the strain shows up in the joints as pain, stiffness or limited range in movement. Imbalances cause the soft tissues to accumulate fiber in the muscle and surrounding fascia for additional

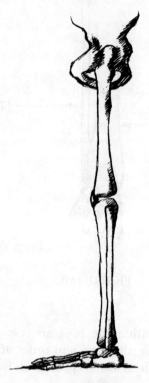

FIGURE 17
Balanced "stacking" of the hip, knee, and ankle hinges.

support. This reduces the free movement of fluid through the tissues. A loss of fluid movement means that oxygen and vital nutrients in the blood cannot reach the cells efficiently and metabolic waste products are not properly eliminated. As the tissues increase in density, there will be a proportionate reduction in the ability of the legs to perform their "second heart" function. As the fluids from the legs meet increased resistance, blood pressure will rise and the body has to work harder than it is accustomed. This leads to a constellation of all too familiar problems, i.e., vulnerability to injury due to progressive displacement of structure — resulting in a loss of mobility and compensating by other body areas. The domino effect has begun.

A man who is a retired Army officer came to be Rolfed at the suggestion of a friend. He mentioned that he had been having problems with high blood pressure for the last six years. For three years his doctor had been regularly prescribing medication to manage his blood pressure. His legs were extremely tight and appeared rather small for a man of his size (6'1" and 190 lbs.). In the second session we began working on his legs. They were incredibly rigid, with dense areas of connective tissue built up at the ankle and on the outside of the knee. The muscles on the outside of his lower leg felt like they were frozen to the shin bone. "Maybe some of this tightness came from the many hours of standing at attention during parades and inspections," he said. It appeared that the man's whole body was still at attention and his legs were working the hardest of all. It was after the eighth session that he returned to his doctor for a check-up. His doctor was amazed — "Your systolic has dropped 22 points and the dyastolic has dropped 16 points. Keep using your medication, it really seems to be working now!" (He had discontinued his medication after the third session of Rolfing, as the pressure in his legs began to release and he started feeling better.)

In order to function normally, the foot, ankle, knee and hip hinges must be "stacked" on each other and their related soft tissues must be properly balanced. Imbalances create twisting and shearing forces through the joints. Any failure in a local part of this system will be transmitted through the neighboring joints. Like gossip in a small town, nothing stays local for long in a body. The fibula and the small bones of the foot are regularly mobile and adaptable. As mentioned earlier, the fibula is secured only by ligament and muscle, with no bony socket or notch to give it an absolute position. The foot is held in position by ligaments and muscles. This arrangement allows the foot to be highly adaptable, whether the demand is to handle weight from above or to respond to the changing contours of the ground. The relationship between the femur and the tibia is a relatively secure one. The knee joint has deep bony contours and strong binding ligaments and muscles that keep it from becoming unstable. Under stress this is the last joint in the leg to modify its function/structure. When the more mobile foot and lower leg use up their capacity for absorbing imbalance, the strain will move to the knee and surface as "knee trouble." If the knee trouble resulted from compensation over time, then the Rolfer would work on the compensation in the lower leg to relieve the knee strain. If the knee was strained because of a direct injury, then the Rolfer would also work more directly on that area.

Let's look at the bony arrangements found in some common foot and leg patterns. We usually recognize a "flat foot" if the inner arch is too close to the ground. Refer back to the drawings of the arch structure and see that both the inner and outer arches are supported by a common point at the heel. (Figure 18A) The position of the heel plays a major role in the strength of the arch. It is not likely to have a flat foot unless the heel bone (calcaneus) has moved out to the side from under the top bone of the foot (talus). As the inner arch fails, due to lack of heel alignment, there is a corresponding inward rotation of the tibia. As part of the flat foot pattern, the fibula may move forward or back, up or down, depending on changes in the position of other weight segments higher up in the body. The opposite of a flat foot is an extremely high arch. A high arch is often confused with a "good" arch, although it is usually troublesome due to its lack of flexibility. The heel is again the key to this pattern. In this case it will be drawn inward in relation to the talus and the lower leg, throwing the weight strongly to the outside of the foot. Depending upon the positioning of the structures above, the femur and tibia may be rotated in or out on their long axes. (Figure 18B)

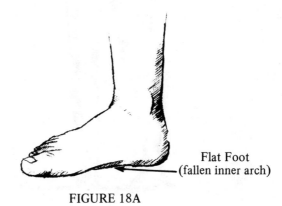

Flat Foot
(fallen inner arch)

FIGURE 18A

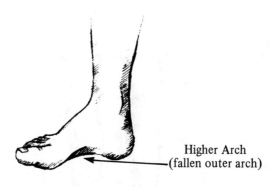

Higher Arch
(fallen outer arch)

FIGURE 18B

Another pattern of adaptation is know as "pigeon toes." (Figure 19A) A more accurate term would be pigeon legs as this pattern actually starts at the groin and involves inward rotation of the whole leg. The opposite of pigeon toes is the "slew" or "duck" foot. (Figure 19B)

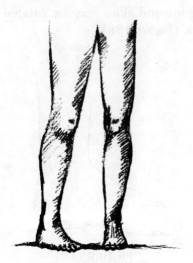

FIGURE 19A
Pigeon Foot

FIGURE 19B
Slew or Duck Foot

In this case the upper leg is often rotated in at the groin, but the lower leg is strongly turned out below the knee. The point here is that specific areas of displacement must always be evaluated in relation to their effect upon neighboring body parts. I have many clients, who as children were treated for misaligned feet (club foot, flat feet, pigeon toes). The apparent problem was "corrected" by casts or night braces, etc., only to surface as spinal rotation or curvature in later years. If only one component of structural imbalance is addressed, other segments of the body will absorb the transferred imbalance.

The leg bone connects to the pelvis at the hip. Looking further we see that the leg does not end at the hip, either structurally or functionally. Rolfers consider a broader definition of a joint to include the joint itself as well as every structure that crosses it or is related to it in movement. The "legs" extend to the bottom inner surface of the ribs via the psoas muscle. The psoas major and minor and iliacus are known collectively as the "psoas" (pronounced "sew-as"), or iliopsoas, muscle. The psoas spans a wide range of depths and segments as it traverses from the inside of the upper leg to the inside of the upper lumbar vertebrae and lower ribs. Because it forms a "bridge" between the legs and the upper body, its tone and vitality affects a wide range of functions. Major nerve trunks from the spine cross and pass through portions of the psoas, involving it in the well being of the respiratory system, digestive system, eliminative and reproductive systems, and basic locomotor functions of the lower extremities. (Figure 20) When the tone of the psoas is balanced with the surrounding muscles the hip hinge will function properly as leg movements are able to transmit all the way to the spine. The ability of the legs to transmit a wave of movement through the pelvis to the rest of the body will be disrupted if the related muscular or skeletal components are imbalanced. If the psoas is balanced, the knees will

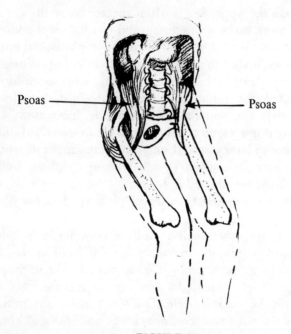

Psoas ——————————————— Psoas

FIGURE 20
The psoas is still a mystery to most. When it is activated and balanced with surface abdominal muscles a person will feel its significance during movement.

track parallel and straight ahead. Without balance in the
psoas, we see a "rolling" or "jerky" gait with lots of side
to side movement which impedes the intended line of
travel. The key to evoking balance in the psoas lies in the
tracking of the knees. If the knees are tracking parallel,
the psoas will spontaneously follow this normal line of
movement. If a person tries to control the tracking of their
feet while their knees are still imbalanced, this will tend to
lock up the function of the psoas, resulting in less efficient
patterns of movement. In addition, existing imbalances
and rotations will simply be shoved higher into the body,
perhaps to the pelvis or spine, similar to what happens

when corrective appliances are placed on the feet.

Perry has been dancing professionally for eleven years. Some of his training has focused on consciously using the psoas in movement:

"I've been to numerous classes and workships where a lot of attention was focused on using the psoas in dance. But I never really saw others use it in their movement, and I can't honestly say I had a real good sense of it in my own body. It's still kind of a mystery to most dancers I know. Since being Rolfed I have a living experience of the psoas and use it actively, relieving my outer muscles from overwork. It's a quiet but very powerful place from which to move."

SHOES

When a client comes in complaining of back pain, the first thing a Rolfer will check is the kind of shoes they are wearing. The original intent behind putting on a shoe was to protect the foot from the abrasive surface of the ground and from extremes of temperature. The foot was designed by a master architect. It is built to respond to the surface under it and to the pace and attitude of the body's movement. This puts some rather definite limits and absolute criteria on the design of a shoe that is to "work." People are often more concerned with the appearance of their shoes than with their functional quality. It is possible to get shoes in just about any shape or design. We have negative heel shoes, or high heels. We have wooden shoes that don't bend at all or flexible pumps to wear to a ball. You can get a cowboy boot with a wedge sole or with a high arch and riding heels. The variety is endless — not so the feet that must fill these shoes.

The human is a multi-gaited animal. When we are walking or trotting the foot ideally hits on the center of the heel, transfers to the metatarsal arch, and then pushes off from the ball to the toes.[1] Ideally, the movement tracks fairly straight through the foot without much side to side wobble. As we pick up speed we drive less energy through the heel and move more toward our toes. At a full sprint we can run on our toes and not contact the heel at all. We are the only creature in the world that has developed an arch for itself. The arch must be allowed to function in a shoe if we are to move with any grace at all. To build a shoe that does not permit the arch to work would be like making gloves without thumbs. If the shoe disrupts the hinge action of any of the joints involved in walking it will reduce the level of function of the whole body.

The following points may help you when you're buying shoes:

1. They must have room for the spring and rebound of the arch. Do the shoes press up into your inner arch and make your body weight fall to the outside of the shoe? Don't get them!

2. They must support and allow hinge function in ankle to heel and ankle to tarsal joints. Walk 5 minutes in the shoes before you buy them. If you can't feel a hinging action in the ankle, they aren't for you.

3. They must permit the smooth transfer of movement to proceed at all gaits. (Can you run to catch a bus in these shoes?)

4. They must allow the foot to respond to changing

---

1.   Tabor, James, "Walking: Focus on Motion", Backpacker Magazine, pp. 40-49, April/May 1981.

contours. Wooden soles, clogs, etc. do not allow responsiveness in the foot.

Obviously there are time when one's occupation will dictate the need for specialized footwear. A heavy construction worker might need steel-toed boots to protect the foot from injury. A "laden" walker (postal carrier) might want extra support for arch and ankle, while a fashion model might want four-inch heels to accent her calves or the shape and length of a garment. Someone with poor arches may want additional support from a shoe insert, but the average person, with functional legs and feet and no unusual occupational demands, should be looking for footwear that meets the basic criteria just outlined. If worn habitually, shoes that modify the angle of the foot's meeting with the ground will eventually cause the whole body to adapt. It has already been pointed out that the body can arrange its connective tissues to "splint"[2] an unusual pattern. The constant "downhill" movement of high heels or "uphill" pattern of negative heels may cause major changes, from simple postural adaptations to crowding or straining of internal organs that are never supported by the hinges (pelvis, knees) below them.

A client I worked with is 5'2" and slightly overweight. She is very conscious of her height and has been wearing high heels since she began working at a C.P.A. firm at the age of 18. Now at age 28 she has constant pain in her low back. In addition, the high heels were actually making her body shorten because of the compensations it made in order to balance on four-inch "stilts." Her neck began to get very stiff and more often than not she had a headache. After Rolfing, she gained new self-confidence and began

---

2. Splinting is the body's response to accumulated stress, in which more fiber is added in an effort to give support to the tissues receiving the majority of the strain.

focusing less on how tall she was. She actually regained 1½" in length because of her new alignment and because she stopped wearing the high heels which were the main cause of her structural distress. She reports "even if I'm not real tall I sure feel a lot taller and lighter. My posture has improved significantly and I feel good about myself."

It is recommended that regardless of what shoes are in style, you "go conservative" in the interest of ease and preservation of balance in the body. Fashion footwear is all right for special occasions, but for the majority of the time spent on your feet, wear shoes that are wide enough to allow your feet to comfortably spread out, that have no false arch support and in which the heel is no more than two inches higher than the toe. Keep enough variety in your footwear to avoid having to "adapt" yourself to a particular style of shoe.

SELF HELP

The following tips can help you improve balance, strength, and ease of movement in your legs and feet.[3] First of all, lie down and practice this exercise by imagining the movements once, then proceed to actually doing the walking after you have rehearsed it once or twice with mental imagery. You are walking along on a flat surface in comfortable shoes in an easy gait. Pay attention to how the weight of your body goes through your legs. As you push off your right leg and it swings under you, let your knee track parallel to your imaginary line of travel. The hip should feel loose and fluffy as it swings through and allows the foot to plant on the ground. The key focus is you are swinging the knee straight ahead. This allows for

3.   See Appendix C-1 for more extensive arch exercises.

greater balance in your gait and support for your pelvis during movement. Do not attempt to control the placement of the foot; allow it to follow the direction of the knee. Repeat twice, the first time with your eyes closed, the second with your eyes open.

This single exercise will help to develop a higher level of order in your ankles, arches, and feet. Stand with the feet parallel about 2 inches apart. Place your hands on the back of a chair to help maintain your balance. Your eyes should be focused out in front of you, not at your feet. As in the knee tracking while walking, bend both knees straight forward about 3 inches. Now begin to raise up slowly on your toes so that the weight is focused mainly through the big toe and the second toe, go slowly so the weight doesn't fall to the outside of the foot. This will strengthen the arches while encouraging your knee to pattern straight ahead over the inner aspect of the foot. Repeat the movements ten times, twice a day to start. In a few weeks you will experience an increase in strength and an improvement in the tracking of your knees, ankles, and feet. At this time you can increase the number of repetitions.

6

PELVIS
A Point of Balance

When the pelvis is not balanced, we do not have the upward thrust that creates zero balance, the sense of weightlessness that can be experienced in the body. When the pelvis is aberrated, it does not allow this equipoise, this tranquility in experience that a balanced pelvis shows.

I.P.R.

There are many aspects of ourselves that proceed with little or no intervention. The heart beats, the lungs breathe, temperature is regulated, digestions proceed, and so on. These functions are governed by the autonomic (involuntary) nervous system. There are other functions that we control voluntarily. We decide to take a walk, have a drink, dig a ditch. As we focus our attention on what to do with our lives, our bodies carry on the processes of living whether we are aware of them or not. In deciding to have a glass of water, the act of reaching for the glass is a voluntary action; once swallowed, the process of absorbing the water into the body from the stomach onward is out of our hands. The animal in us has it covered, to the point where the water has been to individual cells, picked up metabolic wastes, filtered through our kidneys, filled the bladder and signaled us that the "drink" is now ready to be released. If it is not convenient to urinate at that time we can postpone it for a while by flexing certain muscle groups, but in a short time it will be imperative that the animal be heard.

We are delicately balanced by our voluntary and our involuntary systems. There is nowhere in the body that this balance has stronger significance than in the pelvis, which contains our organs of elimination and reproduction. In this region, personal bias and cultural taboo (which involve the voluntary system) meet with the animal need and drives (involuntary). The vital rhythms related to reproduction and elimination are vulnerable, subject to the influence of inaccurate beliefs and feelings. It seems that most Americans have a very low level of awareness and a very high degree of contraction in the pelvic region. The so-called "tight ass" seems to be more than a figure of speech. The functions of elimination and reproduction are susceptible to our character and parental and societal influences. Individual needs, future fears and past traumas can cause us to continuously adapt in the pelvis. Here we flex and hold to control the animal, to be appropriate and civilized.

By observing the pelvis we can see how much a person has been able to balance his instincts with his social conditioning. Stan's pelvis appeared under-developed for a man of thirty. An electronics wiz, Stan lived in his mind. He could explain anything technical and figure out solutions to almost any problem. He had a history of ruptures and prostrate problems. His anus was drawn up deeply and covered over by fleshy buttocks. His genitals were retracted and barely visible. Only rarely would he allow a full breath to reach way down into his belly and pelvis. Stan complained of having no energy and couldn't sustain a relationship, mostly because of his feelings of inadequacy in sexual matters. He had said no to his sexual feelings for so long that now he didn't seem to have them any more. With new balance in his body, freedom in his pelvis and integration between the "genius" and "animal" in him, he is now enjoying all aspects of his life more and appreciating his sensual qualities.

A woman in her late forties who I'll call Sharon had a history of trouble in her pelvic area. Her left hip bone was larger than her right. She had one miscarriage and two children who required forceps delivery. Her menstrual cycle was irregular and always quite painful. She often felt pain during intercourse, but was afraid to tell her husband for fear it would disrupt their already tenuous sex life. Sharon was raised a strict Catholic and always felt that a lot of the tension in her pelvis came from the early programming she received from the nuns at boarding school (sex was sinful).

"All my life I've been out of touch with my pelvis. I don't like looking at it or even touching it most of the time. As an adult I'm re-introducing myself to this part of me."

When I worked on different parts of Sharon's pelvis in the 4th, 5th, 6th, and 9th sessions of Rolfing she would invariably begin to weep. As she allowed herself to release further, the sounds would turn to full cries and wrenching in her gut. When she began to feel more comfortable with this area of her body, I noticed a new confidence and self-esteem beginning to be expressed. The flush of new energy released from her pelvis became the foundation for a new recognition and actualization of personal power and freedom. She remarked

"I realized I wasn't the fragile little girl that most people wanted me to be. I'm really a very strong, resilient woman."

People wear their character in their flesh. To a trained eye, much of a person's character is revealed by the structure and movement of their bodies. More than anywhere else in the body, a Rolfer looks at the pelvis to evaluate the level of balance between the involuntary and voluntary lives. The pelvis will express the unique way that we have learned to deal with life. It is the delicate interplay between involuntary and voluntary functions that makes this region susceptible to an imposition of character on structure. To exercise control over involuntary body functions, it is necessary to tense areas in the pelvis.

The pelvic basin is the general center of gravity (keystone) in the body. The bony pelvis has three joints — two sacro-iliac joints and the pubic symphysis. (Figure 21) These joints allow for a certain amount of mobility of the hip bones around the sacrum. Unfortunately, this mobility can also play a role in taking the pelvis away from its normal alignment. People who practice bony manipulation, like chiropractors and osteopaths, spend a great deal of time trying to maintain these pelvic joints in their proper positions.

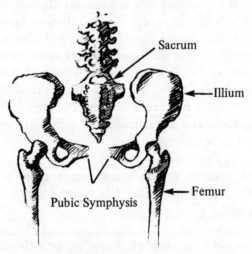

FIGURE 21
These 3 pelvic segments, sacrum and 2 illia are dependent upon the pulls from the soft tissues attaching to them for their proper positioning.

The pelvis is supported by the legs, which rest in the socket of each hip. The spine rests between the hips, with the sacrum acting with the spine and the hips (ilia) with the legs. As we begin to add muscular and visceral components to our map of the pelvis, we see how it becomes a very busy intersection. From the drawings we see that many structures cross and/or insert into the pelvis. Many physiological and mechanical functions take place in and through it. Many feelings (both acknowledged and unacknowledged) reside here. It is not the function of this book to explain in detail the complex nature of the pelvic structure, but the following summary should help give you a general picture of this complex area.

There are three primary muscular layers mostly concerned with connecting the pelvis and legs. The most superficial layer includes the quadriceps, hamstrings, and adductors. Included at this level are the outer abdominal muscles in the front and the spinal muscles and fascia in the back. The muscles which rotate the leg form the middle layer. They start at the top of the leg and travel under the buttock muscles and insert along the back of the pelvis. The deepest muscle layer comes from the leg and crosses the pelvis to anchor within it or onto the front of the spine. This layer includes the obturator internus, piriformis, and iliopsoas[1] muscles. All these layers of connection — pelvis to leg (outer layer), leg to middle pelvic structures (middle layer) and leg to spine (deep layer) must be balanced in order to maintain proper positioning of the organs in the pelvis and for the well being of the entire body. (Figures 22A-B) Poor pelvic alignment increases the possibility of disturbances in organ function. This also works in reverse, as dysfunction in pelvic organs may (by way of reflex)[2] create structural imbalances.

1. See the chapter "From The Ground Up" for a detailed dicussion of the iliopsoas complex.
2. Reflex: A process of one effect continuing from its origin to affect another region of the body.

A client was being treated for kidney problems by his internist; at the same time he began a series of Rolfing sessions. I began to realize that every time his kidneys flared up he also had an increase in pain and discomfort in his lower back. As his kidney condition improved and his body began to release the strain, his low back and hip began to respond to the Rolfing more effectively. The improvement in both kidney function and low back stability mirrored or paralleled one another.

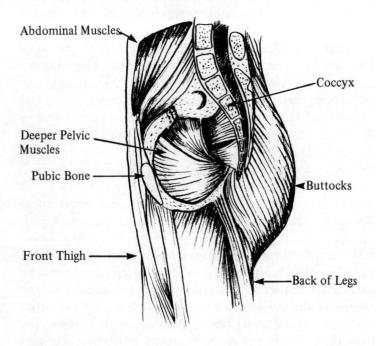

FIGURE 22A   Side View

This drawing shows some of the surface muscles connecting the legs to the pelvis and deeper pelvic muscles which influence leg movement and position spinal and pelvic bones.

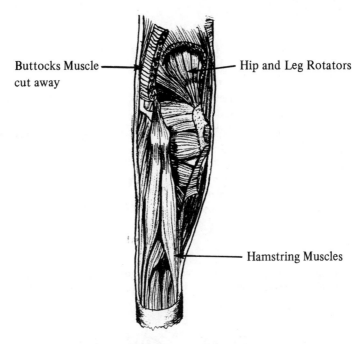

Buttocks Muscle cut away

Hip and Leg Rotators

Hamstring Muscles

FIGURE 22B   Back View
Leg and Pelvic Muscles

The pelvic organs may receive pressure from above (diaphragm and abdominal organs) as well as imbalances from the legs below. If the ribs and diaphragm are compressed, the abdominal organs can get pushed down into the pelvic cavity, creating further problems from pressure and lack of space. (Figures 23A-B) In men, this crowding may cause the bladder and prostrate to become congested and fail to operate effectively. In women, the uterus may become malpositioned with urethra and vagina tilted forward, straining and weakening the pelvic floor muscles. I feel that deterioration of structure and the malfunctioning of female organs has caused too many women

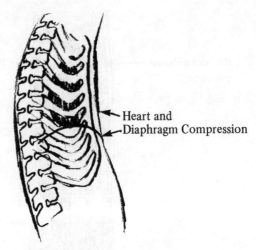

FIGURE 23A

A compressed spine and ribs will crowd the abdominal organs into the pelvic cavity. Structure and function are inseparable.

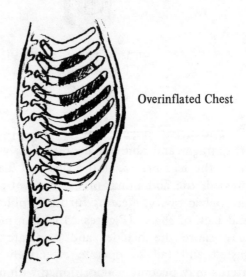

Overinflated Chest

FIGURE 23B

This is fairly good body mechanics with proper spacing of ribs and position of the heart. Still, this person overinflates the ribs and doesn't exhale completely.

to have hysterectomies which perhaps could have been avoided with proper structural alignment. Rolfing balances the pelvis with the surrounding musculature, directly influencing the function of the organs within it.

The work of Dr. Arnold H. Kegel has been reported in a book entitled *The Key to Feminine Response in Marriage*.[3] Basically, Kegel states that the tone of the muscles of the pelvic floor, especially the pubococcygeus muscle, is extremely important to a woman's level of well-being. Muscle fibers in the pelvic floor need to have a balance of tone and span.[4] The span of the soft tissue will of course affect the positions of the bones and vice versa. For example, in the case of the pubococcygeus inserting into the coccyx, any number of impacts (childbirth, a fall on the tailbone, etc.) can change the position of the coccyx. This in turn will unbalance the tone of the pubococcygeus, leading eventually to problems with bladder control, sexual responsiveness, fertility, and childbirth. (Figure 24) If the pelvic floor muscles are in good tone, labor and childbirth will require less effort and there will be less likelihood of tearing the tissue. Also there are no nerve fibers in the tissue of the vagina, so any sensation felt during intercourse is largely dependent upon the health and tone of the pelvic floor muscles around the vagina, especially the pubococcygeus. Like any muscle in the body, this one will perform better when it is exercised and toned.

When a client named Sarah came to be Rolfed she had not had a period in over two years. She also said that sex was not satisfying and that in eight years of sexual activity she had never experienced a complete orgasm. In sessions 4, 5, and 6 we focused upon the structures which shape and support the pelvis. In some areas of her pelvis Sarah was extremely tight and tense, while in other regions

---

3.   Ronald M. Deutsch, New York, Random House, 1968.
4.   See glossary for definitions of span and tone.

her tissue was flaccid and lacked healthy tone. The Rolfing sessions began to balance these discrepancies in tone and the health of her pelvis began to improve. After the 5th session, Sarah reported that her period had started and about one month later she reported a very significant increase in sensation during sex and had experienced regular, deep orgasms.

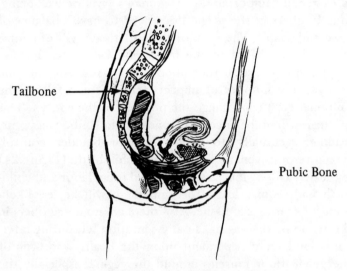

Tailbone

Pubic Bone

FIGURE 24   Side View
This drawing shows good tone and span of the pelvic floor soft tissues and appropriate positioning of lower spine and pelvic bones.

Let's examine what a pattern of flexion might look like in the pelvis. How will the pelvis dramatize our character? The pelvis has a range of front to back movement around the head of the femur. Patterns of flexion occur at the poles of this movement range. (Figure 25) If a person is flexed around the genitals, they will draw in this region, tipping the pelvis forward and deepening the curve in their

FIGURE 25
The ball and socket joint in the hip allows for a wide range of movements by the leg.

lower back. This can cause the thighs to rotate inward, which disorganizes the knee hinges. (Figure 26) If a person is holding around the anus and buttocks, the pelvis will tend to turn back, flattening the lumbar curve. The buttocks would appear to be pinched in and flesh will bunch up around the top of the pelvis. (Figure 27) It is possible that the upper legs would rotate outward, although this leg pattern is not as absolute as described in genital flexion. A retracted anus may not release for a normal bowel movement. If the deep sphincters around the anus are held in a chronically flexed position, there may be a mild extrusion of veins from the anus, which could lead to a full case of hemorrhoids.

In addition to the front/back movements, (Figures

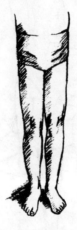

FIGURE 26   Genital Retraction
In a genital retraction the tail (coccyx) tends to tip back and the
front of the legs ride up into the groin.

FIGURE 27   Anal Retraction

28A,B,C) there are also some patterns of twisting, such as the pelvis adapting to a spinal curvature or a so-called "short leg." In this case, the hip no longer sits properly in the socket and the low back rotates to provide additional support. (Figure 28D)

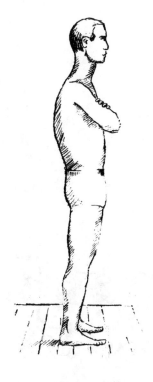

FIGURE 28A

The pelvis has a range of front to back positions. Note how pelvic position will cause a corresponding adjustment in the position of the shoulder girdle.

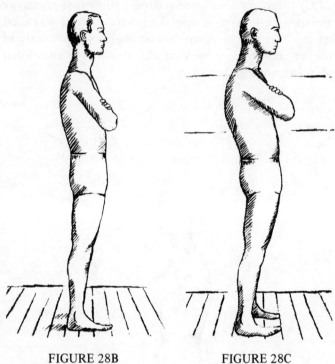

FIGURE 28B   FIGURE 28C

FIGURE 28D
The spine, sacrum, pelvic bones (illia) and leg bones can all be misplaced in a complex interactive pattern. It's not always easy to tell
which of these components started the imbalance but the end result
is almost always pain.

The possibilities for displacement from normal in the pelvis include rotation, twisting, and front/back movements. These are very complex adaptations which are not within the scope of this work. The situations described illustrate general patterns and not absolute conditions. There will always be variations on these themes. Keep in mind that the entire body, in terms of balance, symmetry and tonus, will be affected by these adaptations at the pelvis. We can now appreciate both the complexity and significance of this part of the body and how the major goal of Rolfing continues to be the adjusting of the pelvis toward a horizontal position.

SELF HELP

1. Simple pelvic lift: The goal of this exercise is to lengthen and flatten while making more pliable the lumbar (lower back) curve. Lie on your back with knees up and feet flat on the ground. Take a few complete relaxing breaths, remembering to expand your waist (lower ribs) and thorax side to side and front to back. Be aware of the space behind your lumbar spine. Roll your hips back so the space is smaller and your pubic bone points up toward the ceiling. Hold this position for a count of 10 (don't hold your breath), then slowly let your hips roll forward, returning to the stationary position. Now keeping your tail turned under (hips back, pubic bone up), lift your buttocks off the floor by pushing your knees out in front of you (your buttocks will be 3-5 inches off the floor). Imagine a cable pulling through the knees and out the top of your head. Hold this position for 10 seconds, then slowly, one vertebrae at a time (starting with the vertebrae of the mid back), begin setting the vertebrae back down onto the floor (like the links in a chain),

until the whole spine is back flat on the floor. Do this exercise daily for a healthy back. You can also use it to help when your back (low) or hips are bothering you.

2. This exercise will give you an experience of "getting on top of your legs" by practicing transferring weight across the ball and socket of the hip joint. Stand with your feet comfortably parallel (slightly everted), 3-5 inches apart. Get a general rolling motion going as you rock forward and back, placing most of your body weight on the balls and toes of the feet (visualize the wheels of a train rolling in a forward circle). Try to allow the knees to track in a position centered over the big toes. Now feel the same forward circling motion in the hips as the ball rolls around in its socket (again, visualize the train wheels in the hip joint). First you will have the wheels (hip joints) moving synchronously forward for one minute. Then for one minute have both wheels (hip joints) rolling backwards. (Kind of like an exaggerated yet stationary moonwalk.) Now take these exaggerated actions into movement and begin to walk around the room while you feel the ball and socket action in your hip joints and at the joints that attach the pelvic bone to the spine (at the sacrum). Allow the reverberations from this motion to flow up your spine right out the top of your head. Now you are moving with well-oiled and stacked (aligned) hinges which share the responsibilities of movement.

7

TORSO / ABDOMEN
Breathing and Feeling

When the position of the ribs is changed, breathing changes. In the first hour of Rolfing, if we start on the right side, the client will feel the right side is breathing differently. He'll feel he's getting half again as much air up through the right side.

I.P.R.

A young woman came to get Rolfed with complaints of "low energy and poor posture." Her chest was deeply sunken, creating a very hollow cavity between her breasts. Her head and neck were jammed down and carried forward and her shoulders slouched forward also. She became depressed quite easily and felt that she was too submissive in her relationships. Direct manipulation of the chest and upper back softened her sunken pattern. Often due to the marriage of character and structure release of this area will sometimes be reflected in attitude changes, especially greater self-esteem or a reduction of "over prideful" attitudes and behavior. Halfway through the sessions she reported a new sense of confidence and ease in interpersonal relationships.

A client named Phillip came in to be Rolfed and reported that he was in "good shape" and his only complaint was a little neck and low back pain. Phillip talked a lot about his father and the pride he had in his body. He brought a picture of his father to one of his sessions, it was similar to Phillip's picture. Phillip is always in control. His chest appears over inflated and he never seems to let down his guard. Everything is experienced as a challenge. He never slows down or relaxes and he gets angry when people don't appreciate his accomplishments. Phillip's chest feels rigid when you touch it, as if his breastbone was made of wood. After working nearly an hour on his chest I could finally feel it beginning to soften a little. Small tears began welling up in his eyes when he said

"I haven't even thought of crying since I was about twelve. I didn't realize I was covering up this sadness. I've never seen my father cry, not even at Grandpa's funeral."

Although these two clients' patterns (sunken/collapsed, rigid/inflated) were at opposite ends of the spectrum, both chest patterns were used to protect their fragile inner contents. Phillip's pattern was simply more aggressive and gave the appearance of a healthy condition.

Rolfers are drawn to aspects of structure as indicators of how healthy a person is in terms of body condition and disposition. When we look at someone, much of our attention is drawn to the shape of their ribcage (torso) and stomach (abdomen). The surface contours or shapes tell us the condition of the underlying structures as well as the general attitudes which they embody. When we see a person with their chest held high and their stomach pulled in and flat, our reactions may range from seeing them as "fit" and "in good shape" to their being "prideful" or "stuck up." At the other end of the postural spectrum, a person with their chest collapsed and stomach protruding will be seen as in "poor shape" or lacking vitality, with low self esteem, or even a hostile character. From this point of view, both ends of the posture spectrum described above represent departures from normal. The relationship of torso and abdomen have an optimum form which includes a balanced relationship of major segments, adequate internal space for breathing, and proper placement and functioning of the organs. When organs are compressed through tension or poor posture, their efficiency is lowered as they respond to the displacement. This shows the intimate relation between body structure and organ function.[1]

The torso and abdomen are divided into two compartments by the diaphragm, a muscular "tent" attached to the bottom of the ribcage. (Figure 29) Above the diaphragm are the heart and lungs which are respectively concerned with blood circulation and the exchange of gases between the body and its environment. Below the diaphragm are the "bowels." Their major functions are the processing of food, elimination of waste and filtration of the blood. The upper compartment in the torso is shaped by the span of

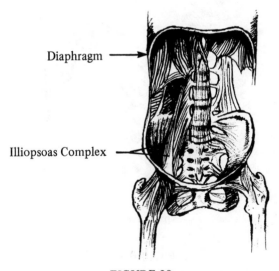

Diaphragm

Illiopsoas Complex

FIGURE 29

1.   See Joel Goldthwait, *Body Mechanics in The Study and Treatment of Disease*, J. P. Lippincott, Philadelphia, PA, 1934, for a complete discussion of the relationship between structural imbalance and organ dysfunction.

the ribs that encircle it and by the diaphragm below. Each rib is attached to a vertebrae in the spine by a movable joint. In the front of the body, only the first seven or eight ribs attach to the breastbone (sternum). (Figure 30) The ribs below the sternum are indirectly attached to it by the cartilage which is springy enough to allow mobility and tough enough to secure the rib ends. The diaphragm is attached to the inner surfaces of the lower ribs. Proper spacing of these ribs helps the diaphragm to compress and expand the space inside the ribcage as we breathe.[2]

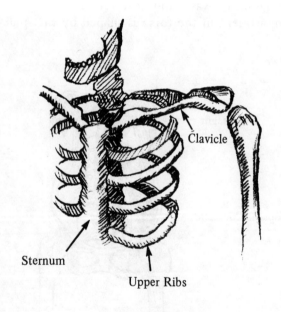

Clavicle

Sternum

Upper Ribs

FIGURE 30

2.   There are many schools of thought on appropriate breathing techniques. The goal is not to impose a particular pattern of breathing, but rather to free structures of respiration so they may function optimally.

From the pelvis upward the ribcage is supported by
long spinal muscles that run from the top of the hips to
the base of the skull. (Figure 31) Fibrous bands and muscles position the ribs, assist in the movements of breathing
and help to maintain space in the chest. The last two ribs
are attached to the spine, but their front ends are not attached to the breastbone. These floating ribs serve as an anchor for the lower fibers of the diaphragm. (Figure 32)
They are often jammed together in odd positions which
hinder normal breathing. In the torso, the heart, lungs and

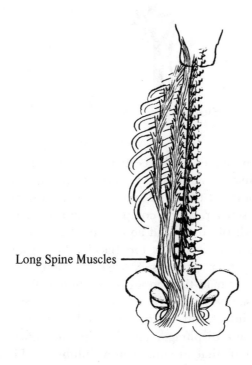

Long Spine Muscles ➝

FIGURE 31

Rear View

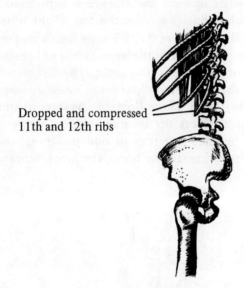

Dropped and compressed
11th and 12th ribs

FIGURE 32

associated tubing are all allotted a certain space and position for their optimum functioning. Failure of tone in soft tissues will let the angle of the ribs down, making the upper organ "container" smaller, which compresses and restricts the contents of both the torso and abdomen. If the abdominal space is too compressed or too flaccid the organs will be jammed together. (Figures 33A-B) The other extreme, with the body held tight in a classic "military" or ballet position, usually keeps the form of the internal space more or less intact, but the rigidity and holding will freeze up the ribs and diaphragm and flex the abdominal contents to the extent that function will be inhibited. (Figures 34A-B) Appropriate spacing in the torso and abdomen will allow for proper functioning of the organs. In addition to supporting good posture and housing the organs, the torso/abdomen is an area where great emotional activity is experienced. In the upper cavity we have the heart, a sensitive monitoring network for all emotions. Our "hearts" are open when we are sensitive and tend to close down when we are insensitive. The "things of the heart" include feelings of joy, love, intimacy and inner spaciousness on the one hand, and sadness, separation, "closing down", and a longing for affection and security on the other.

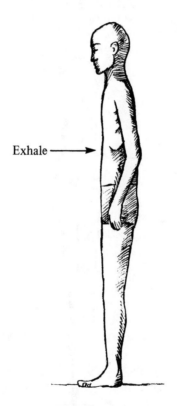

FIGURE 33A

Although very "needy", this type of person finds it hard to be assertive, to ask for what they want. They find it hard to take in a full breath for fear of being overwhelmed by the sensations.

FIGURE 33B

A dropped diaphragm and compressed chest will crowd the normal spacing of the abdominal organs.

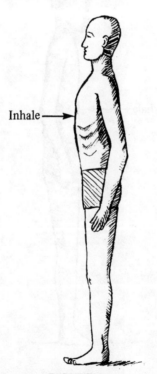

Inhale⟶

FIGURE 34A

This type of person finds it hard to let down his guard, to exhale fully, all the while trying to protect an over prideful and sensitive character.

FIGURE 34B
A pulled up diaphragm, chest, and upper ribs will "freeze" the normal movement and functions of torso/abdomen muscles and organs.

A client came for Rolfing with one of his chief complaints being chest pains. He had a full cardiac exam but was told all was well. While working on his chest I felt as if his heart and lungs were strongly compressed. I began working between his lungs right over his heart, trying to allow the organ to free up a little. He became very scared and pushed my hand away. "I'm sorry," he said, "it felt like I couldn't get a deep enough breath, like a heart attack maybe." Just then he burst into tears and began to make child-like cries and moans. He then talked about how he has felt unattractive all his life and how his heart ached for feelings of affection and closeness from another.

"I was always the ugly one in our family — glasses from age four, slightly paunchy, no good at sports, never any dates in school — so I spent most of my time studying. I used to be obsessed with finding someone who would love me and appreciate me for who I am. I've kind of tried to forget that idea and enjoy life as best I can."

As his ribcage eased he reported on several occasions that he was feeling more outgoing and that he had lost his temper at work and had confronted an employee who was chronically late and somewhat sloppy in her work. This was a breakthrough for him and when he came for his last session he asked about the advisability of taking up tennis or racquetball to keep in shape. He was feeling very good about himself, and wanted to try exercise for his own enjoyment.

In addition to the heart we also have the lungs in the upper cavity. Different patterns of breathing dramatize many feelings and personality characteristics. Some people are "caught" on inhale, finding it difficult to exhale, to return what is given. Such people tend to be outgoing, generous, expressive and can also be overbearing and miss others' more subtle communications. (Figure 35) The polar type of this are those who are caught on the exhale phase. They are slouched forward and their backs are wrapped around them like a cloak. These individuals have trouble taking things in. They tend toward passivity and experience a lack in their world. (Figure 36) Both of these extremes result in lessened vitality, exaggeration of spinal curves, inhibition of movement and breathing and reduction of available space in the torso/abdomen. The torso can be freed from getting stuck in either pole. Most people are amazed at how much better they can breathe after only one session of Rolfing. A 34-year old client that I'll call Karen was born one month prematurely, with the umbilical cord wrapped tightly around her chest and neck. She has a history of upper respiratory problems, including pneumonia, bronchitis, laryngitis, shortness of breath and chronic colds.

"I don't believe I've ever taken a really full breath until after my first Rolf session — then it felt as if a fifty pound weight was lifted from my chest. Breathing used to be such a chore — now it is pure delight."

Exhale

FIGURE 35

Inhale

FIGURE 36

In the abdomen, or belly, we experience our "gut level" feelings and instinctual needs for sex, food and survival. Because there is no skeletal protection, the vital organs of the belly are exposed and vulnerable. Our deepest anxieties, our awareness of self, others and environment all combine to give us the sense that life is "O.K." or that life is basically threatening. When Rolfers work around the belly many people become very "touchy" and find it hard to relax and let go. Most are unaware of how they have been gripping tightly in their guts and how such tightness inhibits spontaneous feelings and expressions. It is often with our guts that we respond strongly to others and to our own needs as well. Healthy aggression allows us to reach out and get what we want from the world in an affirmative way. If this natural aggression is stifled, hostility and spitefulness will occur. It is from our belly that we can give in to our non-rational self if the urge is strong enough and to cry or get mad or be joyful. If the diaphragm and belly wall are held in chronic contraction, it will be more difficult to acknowledge these deeper callings. If these structures are relaxed and receptive, instinctual urges will be naturally expressed in response to the experience of our lives, without risk of either exploding inappropriately from the compressive attitudes or swallowing our feelings endlessly to the extent that life is suffocating.

SELF HELP

1. To have a greater structural awareness of your torso and abdomen, stand in profile (clothes off) to a mirror and observe the relationship of your ribcage to your abdomen and your abdomen to your pelvis. Is the weight and position of the ribcage centered over the pelvis and hip joints? Are you leaning too far back or too far forward? With small rocking motions forward/

back and side-to-side, make subtle adjustments in the position of your ribcage until it feels and appears more balanced over the pelvis. Now go for a short walk and see how your gait has been affected with only the slightest changes. Is your stride lighter, more symmetrical in the tracking of your knees? Has the stride lengthened or shortened? Are you seeing more of the world with a change in the horizon point of your eyes? Even a minor change like this will challenge your old postural habits and feel odd to you. Initially most people feel like they are slumping because the position of the ribcage will be somewhat forward. A quick check in the mirror will show you that your alignment is much straighter. Give your structure and nervous system 3-4 weeks to adjust and you will find that the "old" posture will be the one that feels odd.

2. Lie on your back with the top of your head facing north. Shoes and socks off with feet 8-10" apart. Take a few deep, relaxing breaths. Now place one hand over your head and one hand over your sternum (middle of your upper chest). This time as you inhale, fill out the top hand and then let the air flow out and fill out the bottom hand (feel the belly fill and puff up like a balloon) as you exhale. Let the lower jaw relax and mouth hang slightly open. On the exhale allow a sound or sigh to be released in coordination with the exhale. Continue this bellows action of filling and lifting the top and emptying and rising the lower belly for about 10 minutes. You may be a bit spacy after this so do some gentle pelvic rockers for one minute by lifting the pelvis and allow it to "drop" to the bed until your head clears.

8

ARMS / SHOULDER GIRDLE
Are You Carrying The World
On Your Shoulders?

Males are trained, in ball games and all other kinds of games, to organize their shoulder girdle by tightening and pulling the scapulae (shoulder blades) away from the spine. This is the reason why males get such aberrated shoulder patterns.

I.P.R.

The shoulder girdle is a floating yoke including the arms and the bony and soft tissue structures connecting the arms to the trunk. (Figure 37) From the drawings we see that the only bony joint connecting the shoulder girdle to the ribcage is the collarbone (clavicle) by way of the breastbone (sternum). The arms are connected to the body by the tissues that overlay the neck and also through the muscles that cover the upper ribs. The "neck" portion of the shoulder girdle helps to raise and stabilize the arm when detailed hand motions are being performed. The muscles that overlay the ribs are both the strongest and shortest route for transmitting work through the arms, into the body and out to the ground. (Figure 38) From the drawing we see that the attachments of the chest (pectoralis) and the back muscles (latissimus dorsi) must be balanced for arm movement to be effective. When the shoulder girdle is organized and used properly, the neck remains free from involvement in the heavier aspects of arm use. Shoulders that are held in front of, or behind the lateral midline of the body (as in chest high or chest sunken pat-

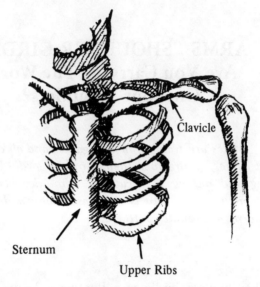

FIGURE 37

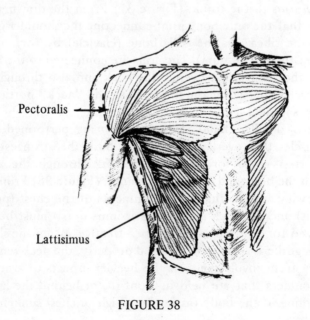

FIGURE 38

terns) will overwork one muscle group in place of another. This will hold true at all levels of effort, from heavy labor to letter writing. The shoulder girdle also functions as a stabilizer for the upright body, in standing and moving. Many people unknowingly use their shoulders to counterbalance exaggerated forward or backward leaning of their bodies. In a common ankle sprain the limping motion is carried all the way to the shoulders. When the ankle finally "heals" we may find that the compensating arm and shoulder pattern does not return to its original state. There is a shadow of a "limp" left over, but this time the limp has an impact all the way to the shoulders.

The upper arm (humerus) bone extends from the shoulder socket to meet with the large bone (ulna) of the lower arm in a hinge joint at the elbow. The smaller second bone of the forearm (radius) lies parallel to the ulna and can rotate on its long axis to provide the wide range of movements characteristic of the hand. (Figures 39A-B) Al-

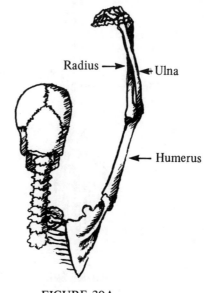

Radius ⟶   ⟵ Ulna

⟵ Humerus

Back View

FIGURE 39A

though we call the structure below the wrist joint the hand,
in structural and functional terms the "hand" is everything
below the elbow, in the same way that the "functional
foot" extends to the knee. The musculature operating the
hand lies along the radius and the ulna, crossing the wrist
to insert at various points in the hand. Finer movements,
like writing, are more local to the forearm, while larger
movements, such as digging or throwing which require
greater range and power, engage the structures closer to
the trunk.

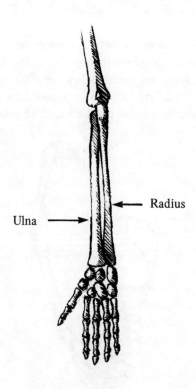

Ulna

Radius

FIGURE 39B

The soft tissue of the shoulder girdle forms in layers over the neck and ribcage. If the outer (extrinsic) muscle layers are rigid and over-developed, comfort and efficiency will suffer. The body will shorten and lose mobility at the deeper levels, in the same way a girdle that is too tight will restrict movement and fluid flow within the abdomen. For balanced development, the deeper tissue layers must have adequate space in which to function. Since both nourishment and cellular elimination flow between deep and surface layers, balance between them is essential.

The outermost layer of the neck just beneath the shoulder girdle turns and supports the head and neck and assists in breathing by lifting and opening the upper ribs. This layer may be involved in respiratory difficulties like asthma, bronchitis, or emphysema. The ribs become fixed in a high position in an attempt to create more space for breathing. In time, the neck muscles will respond to this lack of space by becoming rigid from chronic over-exertion. The shoulders will assume a very square look as the person becomes unable to drop them voluntarily. At this point the body's response to the trouble may actually serve to "lock in" the respiratory problem by reinforcing the posture associated with it.

Larry is a Vietnam veteran with a history of upper chest problems and severe asthma. His voice over the phone sounded hoarse, raspy and far away (like the "Godfather's"!) when he called to make appointments for a Rolfing series. He was receiving injections for the asthma monthly and also had to use an inhalant to keep his lungs open when he had an attack. He appeared as if he had been terribly frightened by something but had never released from this response. His chest was held high and tight, and his diaphragm and solar plexus regions were extremely rigid. After a session of work on the body, he began to relax his chest and breathe more fully. He had a violent asthma attack the next day, but since then has had continual improvement in his breathing. He can now run four to five miles, four times a week.

Edward has been practicing dentistry for many years. His body shows it; his shoulders are stuck tightly to his chest and each of his arms is set differently in the shoulder socket. Because he is right handed and because of the way his equipment is arranged, his right side does most of the fine work. Looking at him in profile or head on, you can see that he leads with his right side. Edward's upper back is quite curved from leaning over the chair. He has frequent neck pain, headaches, low back discomfort and most recently he has begun to feel shooting pains down his arm and stiffness in his wrist joints and fingers. Like many dentists, Edward is very concerned about causing his patients pain. As a result of this concern, he often absorbs a great deal of tension in his body. It is not enough to simply relieve his chronic symptoms. Someone like this needs a complete structural re-balancing and needs to evaluate how they use their bodies and find more effective patterns which balance and support the body to allow ease and efficiency while working. After Rolfing Edward felt great relief from his deep accumulated tension and a new sense of length and ease of movement. He was concerned that his repetitive movement patterns in dentistry would cause his old problems to return. He was referred to a Rolfing Movement teacher who helped him find the most efficient and least tension-producing ways to use his body at work. Edward returns every six months for a tune-up session and reports no recurrence of his old problems.

Aside from the face, the shoulders and arms are the most outwardly expressive part of the human body. From across a room we can get the essence of a conversation by watching people's gestures. By the "set" of the shoulders we can tell the mood of someone coming down the street. (Figures 40A-D) The hands of a storyteller fly about to elaborate and illustrate the unfolding tale. Our language is full of metaphors that point to the importance of this part of our anatomy — "to welcome with open arms," "my hands are tied," "to give a hand" and so on. In the brain there are specialized regions which correlate to each part of the body. It is significant to realize that we have more brain tissue devoted to the thumb than to the whole leg. As a species, this specialization gives us the tool-using capacity that enables us to change the world, for better or worse. Up from all fours, we have our hands free from the job of mobility, free to create or destroy as we choose.

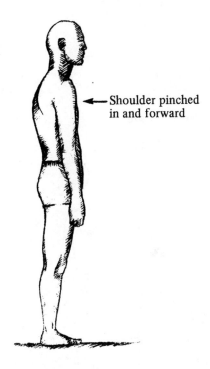

Shoulder pinched in and forward

FIGURE 40A

The shoulder girdle can become stuck in a range of positions front to back, up or down, or too wide or too narrow. It is also interesting to note how these various shoulder patterns can contribute to corresponding changes in the position of the pelvis and low back.

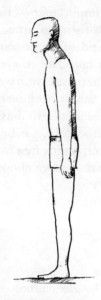

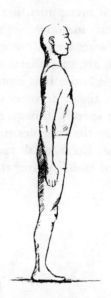

FIGURE 40B

Shoulders pinched in and back

FIGURE 40C

Shoulders up and back

Shoulders down
and forward

FIGURE 40D

If a person's life has been filled with trauma, feelings of sadness, hopelessness or a strong sense of injustice, these will be recorded in their flesh. The feeling of having to "shoulder one's burdens," or to always "carry the load" will be expressed by the set of the shoulder girdle. This over-burdened pattern may also be used to hold back the expression of anger. There may be a fear of striking out and hurting someone, or an inability to say no, or an unwillingness to take charge of one's life. A person in this kind of pattern will often feel physically drained and complain of not having enough energy to take care of their daily "responsibilities." As the strain carried in the shoulders becomes chronic, other parts of the body will begin to contract and hold in order to adapt and support the weakening shoulder girdle area.

Another common structural pattern in the shoulders arises from the misinterpretation or overzealous application of the directive "stand up straight." Children and adolescents are given this command over and over by well-meaning parents and teachers. Often this directive is given without specific information on how to accomplish this, typically without real understanding of the mechanics of good posture. The result is that the child assumes a stance that resembles a military "brace." (Figure 40E) The shoulders, being the most mobile component, are usually pulled back, drawing the shoulder blades (scapulae) together. This gesture may satisfy the adult that the child is trying. The sad truth may be that the "slouch" is a dramatization of the child's emotional attitude. If so, the posture and attitude will be reinforced by the attempts and failures to "stand up straight." The end result could be that the child has a rib pattern that expresses a depressed emotional state sitting under a set of shoulders that are held up and back to "look good." Such a deep structural conflict will create compensations all the way into the legs and feet where the imbalance must ultimately be borne.

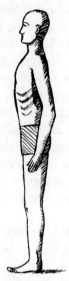

FIGURE 40E
How does your body interpret the directive "stand up straight"?

A nine year old child was brought by his parents to get some structural relief from his slouched shoulders, sway back, and bow legs. Given his present structure he can't stand very well no matter how hard he tries. His stance very much approximates his dad's, who was told by his father to stand up straight. The parents mean well, but like so many other parents, they are concerned with the outward appearance of good posture. They don't fully understand that good structure is the foundation of good posture. External attempts at standing up straight only create more tension and holding in the body, which will lock in the already existing imbalances. As the child's burdened shoulders were released, he told me that he was beginning to feel a sense of lightness in his body, and for the first time he felt standing up straight was not a chore and really felt good.

A balanced pattern in the shoulder girdle and arms will insure comfort, strength, and resiliency in this region of the body. In terms of character, ease in the shoulder girdle expresses itself as the ability to give and receive more readily. In metaphor, the arms are the extension and projection of the heart. We give from the heart, with the hands. We open the hands and arms to receive a gift or embrace our fellow humans. Our uniqueness as humans is clearly expressed through this part of the body. What better reason could there be to seek balance in this area of structure if not to more clearly express the needs of the heart?

SELF HELP — SHOULDER GIRDLE

Finding the place where your shoulders fit best on the ribcage is a little like putting on a coat. Stand in front of a mirror (facing) with your weight evenly distributed over both feet. Take a long, full breath, being especially careful to fill out around the upper ribs and collarbones. You will notice how this automatically lifts and "squares off" the shoulders. Allow the shoulders to respond to the lift from the ribs; don't try and pull them back or stand up straighter. With the shoulders in this easy position let your eyes look out of your head as though viewing a faraway horizon. This will also aid in resting your shoulders and head in a more comfortable and horizontal position. This works best for people whose shoulders wrap around them to the front.

If your shoulders are held back, with the blades pinched together, then your focus will be more on releasing the ribs with a complete exhale. As before, stand facing a mirror and breathe fully into the top and upper sides of the ribcage. As you exhale, allow the weight of the shoulders to fall down onto the ribcage. Instead of you holding the shoulders up and back, you are releasing this job of support to your ribcage, pelvis, legs, and feet. So, as an elevator dropping down to a lower floor, you should have a sensation of the weight of the shoulders falling all the way through your body to the feet. These ideas should help you locate an unstressed position to "wear" your shoulders.

9

HEAD AND NECK
There's More Here Than Meets The Eye

There is no way of separating head and neck; they are one structure. Very oddly, nobody ever seems to think of this. There is no muscle in the face or the head that doesn't reach an anchorage in the cervical vertebrae. That anchorage may be in trouble; it may be too short or too long, too straight or too twisted, but it is there. Things that relate the head to the neck have two ends, one of them is in the neck, and one of them is in the head. As a Rolfer organizes those two ends, you begin to get normal structure.

I.P.R.

The face is our main presentation to the world, the primary vehicle through which we communicate ourselves to our fellow humans. As an important organ of expression, the face is susceptible to a lot of tension. We sometimes smile when we feel it is important to please, even if we don't mean it. We may hold back a grin when we think it inappropriate. There are many expressions in our language that point to this dilemma — "save face," "face it," "bite your tongue," "swallow your feelings," "choke back your anger," and so on. When feelings demanding expression are censored, muscles in the face must be flexed. Imagine all the muscle patterns involved with not speaking your mind. It takes more energy to suppress feelings than to express them.

Although we work on the head and neck throughout

the Rolfing process, there is a session which primarily focuses on the head, neck, face and inner mouth. This work is often accompanied by significant emotional release as well as changes in habitual facial expressions. The manipulation in this area is "close to home" and at times is perceived as threatening. Most of the time this session is experienced as a long overdue opportunity for contacting one's true self and releasing some of the blocks that usually cause us to spend so much of our lives acting the way we think others want us to act. People find themselves speaking their mind more freely or forcefully after this work.

A young woman came to me for Rolfing whose facial presentation could have been summarized in two words — suspicious and bitter. Her eyes were narrow and intense, set deeply in the sockets and continually glaring. Her lips were tightly pressed together and her jaw was firmly set and drawn into her neck. Her jaw and face muscles felt more like steel cables than human tissue. After the face, jaw, and neck work her facial expression relaxed dramatically and she began to have a more positive outlook on life. When she came for her next session, she related the following:

"During that session I felt like the shades were pulled up in a darkened room to reveal a sunny day . . . I'm actually a gentle and somewhat shy person inside, but I've been presenting a fake version of me for twenty-nine years. Finally I'm ready to just be me."

Dr. Rolf used to say "faces are a reflection of necks." Many of the muscles that determine the set of the head and jaw are attached to the front of the neck. If someone came to her with tension and deep "character" lines in their face, she would often work on their necks to relieve the stress residing there. As these contractions were released, their face would become more relaxed and responsive. We have all seen faces that tell us of an underlying character fixation — the down-turned mouth, the furrowed brows, the sneer set into the upper lip. If the tension is occasional or temporary, the muscles can still return to a relaxed state. If the holding becomes habitual, it will be more difficult for the person to release the contracted muscles in their face and neck.

Often the expression of the face suggests a fixed emotional pattern which actually acts as a mask covering the inner most feelings. By looking at a person's face we can sometimes see the central emotional theme around which their life revolves. Other people will give the world the version of themselves they want accepted, all the while their faces belying the truth.

A woman was referred to me by a psychiatrist who was concerned about the woman's long-standing depression which hadn't even responded to medication. Even an untrained observer would look at this woman's body and the expression on her face and see that her life theme was to be suffering. She has been divorced for seven years. For six of those years she has had to support and take care of her mother, who has been slowly dying since her husband passed away eight years ago. Her body appears beaten down. Stuck in an unavoidable situation, she constantly vacillates with important life decisions. She is always "trying to do the right thing" when it comes to others, but she doesn't know how to achieve her own gratification. Her face is locked into a partial smile, but her eyes are sad and lack vitality. Her jaw is undeveloped — suggesting a lack of assertion. Her voice has a whining quality which calls for sympathy. While working around her jaw, her mouth began to quiver and small tears rolled down the creases of her face.

"I'm only forty-seven, but I feel like I've been sen-

tenced for life to take care of my mother. Everyone com-
mends me for being so caring and compassionate — all I
want to do is get away from her. I don't have the guts to
put her into a home. I feel guilty just thinking about it,
but what about me?"

As her ten session sequence drew to a close and her body
came into balanced alignment she saw that many of the
"problems" she had with her mother had a structural
component — they were literally expressing themselves in
the flesh. As the holding patterns began to release, she began to re-evaluate her situation. She devised a more effective system of care for her mother which gave her more
free time and an opportunity to meet some new people.
She was able to "release her problems and turn them into
projects," which required her creative attention.

The position of the head on the neck is influenced by
three layers of muscles and ligaments, running the length
of the spine, from the sacrum to the base of the skull. (Figure 41A) In the layer closest to the bone, small muscles
and "check ligaments" determine the range of movement
between individual vertebrae in the neck. The next layer
forms a series of strap-like muscles which run from the
base of the skull downward and insert into the transverse
processes of the cervical vertebrae (neck bones). A few of
these muscles reach all the way down between the shoulder blades. (Figures 41B,C,D) The third layer runs from
the sides of the cervical vertebrae to the two upper ribs,
stabilizing the neck in front-to-back movement and assist-
ing in turning the head.

The jaw is another area where people store a lot of
tension. This can be in the muscles connecting the jaw to
the head, or in those connecting the jaw to the neck.
Disorder in either of these relationships can be and frequently is the cause of TMJ (temporo-mandibular joint)
problems that may take years to show up.

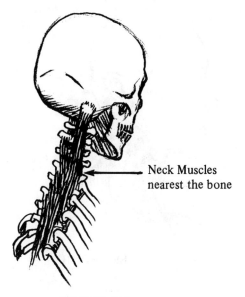

Neck Muscles
nearest the bone

FIGURE 41A

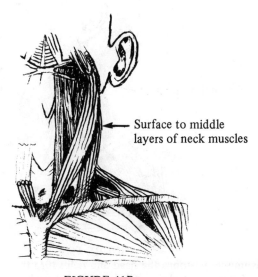

Surface to middle
layers of neck muscles

FIGURE 41B

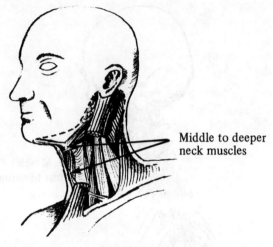

Middle to deeper
neck muscles

FIGURE 41C

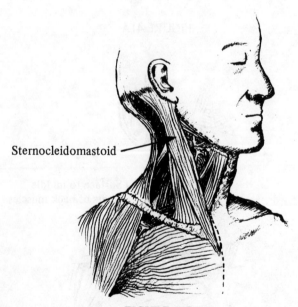

Sternocleidomastoid

FIGURE 41D
This muscle positions the head and helps turn the neck from side to
side. A composite of 3 muscle layers in the neck.

Hank had a long history of neck aches, migraine headaches and tight jaw muscles when he came to get Rolfed.
He had ringing and buzzing in his ears and he ground his
teeth when sleeping.[1] These are all common symptoms of
a condition that physicians call "temporo-mandibular joint
syndrome," or TMJ.[2] The TMJ is the point where the jaw
joins the skull, just in front of the ears. (Figure 42) This
joint is only held together by muscles. These muscles are
used for biting, chewing, talking and in a more general way
are associated with communication. Chronic tension or imbalance in these muscles can be a part of the TMJ problem.
The common procedure for correcting this condition includes the wearing of a splint (which helps to take the tension off the joint) and a slight grinding down or building
up of the teeth to even up the biting surface (equilibra-
tion). Hank's dentist suggested Rolfing after he had his
bite equilibrated. He was still experiencing some headaches and a chronic neck and shoulder pain, although the
dental work had helped a great deal. Hank's neck, jaw, and
shoulder had been a major discomfort for years. The separation and re-organization of these structures through
Rolfing was the key to changing this pattern for the better.
Hank related:

"The work the dentist did really helped a lot, but my
neck and shoulders still hurt and occasionally I got those
awful headaches. After my body was balanced from the
Rolfing, I finally got the relief I had been hoping for."

An imbalanced jaw to head relationship creates tension
in the muscles that run from the jaw to the temples and in
the chewing muscles. Some people chronically clench their

1.   Huggins, Hal, *Why Raise Ugly Kids?* Arlington House Publishers, Connecticut, 1981, discusses sleep positions and TMJ problems.
2.   Gelb, Harold D.M.D., *Clinical Management of Head, Neck and TMJ Pain
and Dysfunction*, W. B. Saunders, 1977.

teeth, which distorts the bite and stresses the teeth in their sockets. This can even compress joints between the various bones of the face and cranium. These compressions can result in ringing and buzzing in the ears, chronic inflammation of the sinuses, recurring headaches, and even vision problems. It's also possible for disorders in the cranium to contribute to or complicate TMJ symptoms. For those people whose TMJ trouble stems from a faulty bite or loss of teeth they should be treated by a dentist who is a specialist in TMJ dysfunction. If the TMJ problems seem to arise "out of nowhere," or could be traced back to an accident, cranial trauma (perhaps from birth) or to whiplash, then I have had best success with a more comprehensive approach including body work, dentistry, and sometimes accupuncture.

One of the most important bones of the head and face is the butterfly-shaped sphenoid which supports the forehead bone and has joints in common with temples, cheekbones, nose and occipital shelf. (Figure 43) The two wings of the sphenoid affect the location of the eyeball by form-

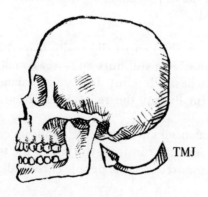

TMJ

FIGURE 42

ing part of the boundaries of the eye socket. Blows to the head and jaw, dental work, sleep patterns and infections in the nasal area can compress or disorganize this critically important bony spacer. This may disrupt the flow of information from the eye to the brain and literally alter the position and shape of the eye. If the sphenoid doesn't maintain normal space between the temporal bones, a number of nerves and arteries can become compressed, reducing the flow to the eyes. The pituitary, or "master gland," secretes hormones which influence our physical and emotional make-up. It rests on the top surface of the sphenoid and can be affected by even a small displacement of the sphenoid.

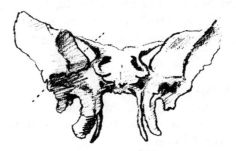

FIGURE 43   Sphenoid Bone

If the primary tensions lie in the connections of the jaw to the neck, where the tongue is anchored, the structural strain will cause the neck to draw forward in relation to the upper body. A person will usually complain of chronic pain at the base of the skull, and may eventually have thyroid[3] related troubles because of the strain in the muscles adjacent to the thyroid gland involved in contin-

3.   The thyroid gland is located in the throat.

ually trying to balance the head on the neck. The deep muscles and ligaments will thicken and shorten in an attempt to relieve strain in the jaw to neck relationship. This tightening ultimately reduces the movement of fluids in the vessels that serve the head and neck.

Adults who experience chronic neck and head pain may have been those who were "seen and not heard" as children. John is such a person. A lawyer, he sought out Rolfing for relief from "head and neck pain that I can't remember not having." John has moved from one firm to another, not having much success. He often seems at a loss for words; not a helpful attribute for someone who must articulate cases for a living. He also complained of digestive problems such as acid stomach, excess gas and constipation. As we began work on releasing his tight jaw muscles he began to cry uncontrollably. Eerie, almost animal-like sounds began to emerge from some distant place within him.

"My parents never allowed us to raise our voices to talk back to them. My dad threatened to whip us with a belt if we pressed our luck. Just think of how much I've swallowed over the years."

John began to consider the possible relationship between his unwillingness to give himself permission to let go (swallowing his words) and his constant problems with digestion. John's body is gradually returning to a state of "not holding" and he seems more willing to express his emotions and not bolt down his food as he used to. All of this is contributing to a more balanced state of being, both structurally (reduced head and neck pain) physiologically (improved digestion) and psychologically (freer expression of emotion).

Head and neck stress can often affect vision. Most schools screen children for vision problems. If they are found to be "abnormal," it is customary to send them to the "eye doctor," who checks the eyes and generally prescribes lenses to correct the vision to "normal." If examined during a time of high stress, when the child may be expressing a problem by "not seeing," the glasses will "lock in" the pattern of not seeing by forcing the eye to adapt to the lens. This is evidenced by the fact that most people who wear glasses do not improve over time, but rather need stronger and stronger lenses as the eyes weaken and become increasingly dependent on the lenses. In addition the lens, by "fixing" the eye, may also lock in the emotional set that the eyes were dramatizing in the first place. I feel that visual problems should be evaluated from a broader perspective. One should look at the set of the child's (or adult's) jaw. Are they breathing normally? How is their home life? How are they adjusting to school? Are they dramatizing an emotional condition in their lives? What are they refusing to see? It is surely not normal to have millions of people wearing glasses. What is going on here? Any lens correction, especially for children, should be accompanied by vision therapy, such as the Bates[4] method, which exercises and educates the eye, allowing the abnormal patterns to unstress and return to normal.[5] Perhaps 2 to 3 eye tests should be done on different occasions to get an "average" reading on eye condition to consider the relation of random stress and vision clarity.

These examples describe the process of stress spreading throughout the body. They also show how body structure, function and character continuously influence one another. If balance is disrupted, the body flexes and shortens the soft tissues and adds fibrous tissue to the stressed

4.   Berret-Rosannes, Marilyn, *Do You Really Need Eyeglasses?* Hart, N.Y., 1974.
5.   See also Developing Eyesight: New Techniques That Improve Visual Skills. Somatics Vol. 5, No. 3, pp. 36-41, Autumn/Winter 1985-86.

areas. If stress is not released there will be compression of joints, nerves and vessels and interference with the free movement of fluids. If this process continues, the body will attempt to spread a localized imbalance over a wider area, locking it into the whole system. The end result creates symptoms, accelerates aging and lowers the efficiency of the whole body.

SELF HELP – HEAD AND NECK

To achieve a place of ease and balance for the head we can create great improvement by shifting the position of the eyes. Stand facing a mirror with your weight distributed evenly over both feet. Check the line of your eyes; are they upward toward the ceiling, are you gazing out from under your brow, or are you "looking down your nose" toward your feet? With a subtle nodding motion scan your head and eyes up and down, blink your eyes occasionally to create a softer view of your world. If the eyes are fixed the head and neck position will also become fixed. Your head should "bob" lightly like a balloon on the end of a string. Don't strain to approximate good posture. The head is a very mobile component of the body and will do much better if it is not held in a static position — let it float! Now begin walking at a moderate pace, letting your eyes look out toward the horizon and allowing your head and neck to float easily and be responsive to the movement of your gait. This should help you to find "home place" for your head and neck.

10

BODY - WORK

We are not truly upright, we are only on our way to becoming upright. This is a metaphysical consideration. One of the jobs of a Rolfer is to speed that process along. We want to get a man out of the place where gravity is his enemy. We want to get him into the place where gravity reinforces him and is a friend, a nourishing force.

I.P.R.

Once a person has been Rolfed, he or she must become aware of their habitual movement patterns in order to sustain and enhance the benefits of their Rolfing. It is important to understand that everything you do in life will either add to or detract from the level of order in your body and your feelings of well-being.

Almost all of us spend a great deal of time at some type of job. With the amount of energy spent working, it makes sense to do our jobs as effectively and efficiently as possible. Specific patterns of movement repeated over and over will reinforce existing imbalances in the body. Attempts to compensate for these imbalances serve to create even more inefficient movement patterns. This increases the possibility of injury, because less movement is available and results in specific symptoms such as low back pain, aching feet, eye strain and other stress-related complaints. New information coming from users of video display terminals suggests we are about to have a new category of chronic musculo-skeletal complaints from people who use these systems regularly.

Roberta works for a University press, using a computerized editing machine eight hours a day, five days a week. She is under a great deal of stress as she has to type and proofread a certain number of pages each hour. She complains of low back pain, tightness in her neck and shoulders, eye strain and almost continual headaches. Because of this pain and physical discomfort, her speed and accuracy have begun to suffer. Her employers have been paying for her weekly visits to a chiropractor for the last nine months. Her body is pushing the limits of stress. Roberta needs complete structural realignment and development of better movement patterns. She got Rolfed and also worked closely with a Rolfing Movement teacher to find a way of working which would not put stress on her body. She changed the position and angle of her chair in relation to the desk where the editor sat. She began wearing headsets to block some of the constant noise coming from all the machinery near her workplace. Her Rolfing Movement Teacher helped her learn how to hinge forward and back from the hip joints instead of bending the head and neck so far forward that it was no longer supported by the torso and pelvis. They also worked on some eye exercises which helped to keep her eyes from "locking up" and "bugging out" while looking at copy all day. She states

"I feel so much better now and really enjoy my work. My boss has rewarded my improved performance by giving me half a day off on Fridays."

Let's look at the effects of various jobs on body structure. By analyzing the body in sitting, standing, and walking positions, we can see how people can feel better by becoming aware of certain principles. Secretaries, truck drivers, airplane pilots, businessmen and policemen find that their occupations require many hours of sitting. In this position the pelvis replaces the legs as the main base of support. When looking at the bones of the pelvis in profile we see that the hip sockets (acetabula) measured at the highest point are nearly in the same plane, or at least they should be if the body is balanced. (Figure 44) It is here that the pelvis assists in supporting the weight of the upper body and creates a basin to contain the internal organs. Imagine someone sitting on a backless bench. In this position the pelvis can be placed in a number of ways that offer varying degrees of stability and support. In the most forward position, the "sits-bones" are moved back and the weight falls on the back of the thigh. This puts the lower back into an extreme forward curve and tips the abdominal contents forward against the inside of the belly wall. The lower back and neck respond by flexing, which increases fatigue. (Figures 45A,B,C,D) The other pole rolls the pelvis to its most extreme rearward position. The weight of the upper body falls behind the pelvis, often straining the sacro-iliac joints and contributing to lower back problems. The pelvis and ribcage are brought closer

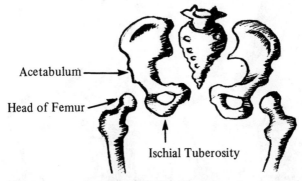

Acetabulum

Head of Femur

Ischial Tuberosity

FIGURE 44

When looking at the bones of the pelvis in profile we see that the hip socket (acetabulum) measured at its lowest point and the "sits bone" (ischial tuberosity) measured at its highest point are nearly in the same plane, or at least they should be if the body is balanced.

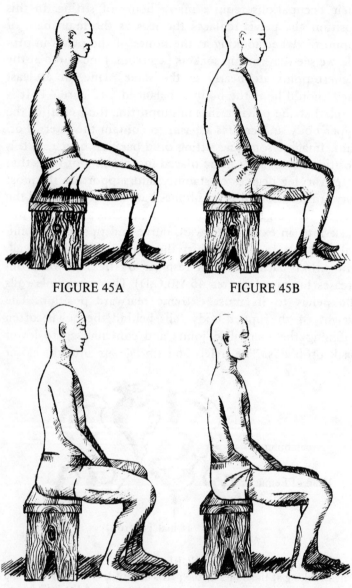

FIGURE 45A   FIGURE 45B

FIGURE 45C   FIGURE 45D
Ranges of Pelvic Positions while sitting

together, which cramps the internal organs. While the forward position creates or dramatizes chronic holding and tension, the rearward position is associated with collapse and failure of support.

These two poles of pelvic position can serve as points of reference as we discuss sitting in chairs and seats. From a structural view, seats should be designed to position and support the body so organs are uncramped and musculature is resilient without undue holding. In chair design, "comfort" should be defined as that which supports the body's order. If you look at the seats in your home, office, restaurants and car, you will see that they are designed to not give the kind of structural support I am talking about. Most seats define comfort as toward lying down. Perhaps this is true for resting, but if your work involves sitting for many hours then adequate support becomes a prime concern. When you sit in a chair ask yourself if the chair allows you to get your pelvis supported under you. (Figure 46)

FIGURE 46
Pelvis in a position to effectively support the body.

Another concern in seating comfort is the relationship
of the legs to the pelvis. For an alert, balanced and supported position, the knees should be no higher than the
hips. Put another way, to ensure support and comfort, the
angle formed by the legs and torso in sitting should be no
more than 90 degrees. If the seat height keeps the knees
too high in relation to the hips, the person is essentially
going in two directions at once. (Figure 47) The high knees
will force the pelvis to roll toward its rearward pole, and in
compensation for this, the person will flex their back and
reach forward with their head. If the person habitually
uses this chair, then they may experience pain or tension
in the lower back, shoulders and neck. Repeatedly sitting
in this position at a job will create eye strain, headaches,
and a build up of tissue around the abdomen, hips, buttocks, and upper thighs. If the legs and pelvis are in the
correct relationship, the person freely balances. The hours
spent working are easier and more effective, as the person
is less fatigued.

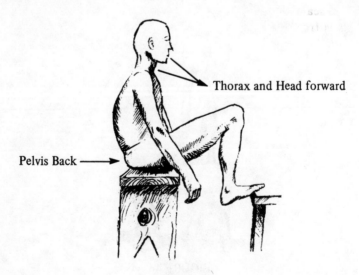

Thorax and Head forward

Pelvis Back ———→

FIGURE 47

Many people have jobs that entail hours of sitting in cars and trucks. A police officer spends a good deal of time riding around in a patrol car with seats that are designed to cradle him in a semi-reclining position. Most American car seats allow the pelvis to turn way under, making it so that you are almost sitting on your spine! How long can anyone be expected to remain alert and responsive in a seat that takes the body toward a reclining position? A sore neck, stiff shoulders and low back pain will soon be the constant companion of those who spend time in poorly designed car seats. One must wonder "who is driving" when it comes to seat design in the auto industry? (Figure 48)

Tony is a regional salesman who drives 800 miles a week on the average. He came to be Rolfed and complained of neck stiffness, eye fatigue, headaches, numbness in his arms and fingers, pain and stiffness in his low back

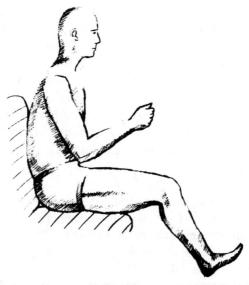

FIGURE 48
Car seats need major re-designing.

and hips and soreness behind his knees. Who wouldn't feel this way after driving 45,000 miles a year in a seat that doesn't support structural balance? After his Rolfing, Tony was virtually pain free and most of his structural related complaints had subsided once his body regained a new level of balance. Next we set out to find ways to make his long distance driving less fatiguing and tension producing. To begin with, we cut a wedge-shaped piece of foam rubber and put it on the car seat to create low back support and encourage the pelvis to stay under the spine. Then we cut another thick piece of foam to be placed on his right thigh as an elbow forearm rest for his right arm. He had been holding that in a continuously cocked position while steering the car on those long open roads characteristic of New Mexico. We then cut another foam wedge which was placed under his knees to allow them to stay relaxed and in a stabilized relationship to his pelvis. All of these changes allowed Tony's body to be relaxed, upright and more alert, while maintaining a balanced posture in the driver's seat. In addition, Tony paid more attention to keeping his breathing free and open, softening his neck muscles and allowing them to be responsive to the shock absorption of the car, and to keep a firm yet relaxed grip on the steering wheel. He began stopping every two and a half hours for a five minute energizer break during which he got out of the car and did some neck rolls, light torso twisting, toe touches and singing to release pent-up energy. Tony reports:

"I used to be bushed after a day on the road and at the end of the week I just had enough energy to eat and lay around all weekend to try and recover. It's still a full day for me, but since my Rolfing I have energy to spare and less of my time is taken up fighting off the aches and pains. Now on weekends I love to go places with my family and plan a little golf when time permits."

For people who work on their feet, such as carpenters, salespeople, technicians and doctors, Rolfing principles can be applied to create greater ease in the body while still improving effectiveness.[1] Again, we look to the body in gravity for our information.[2] The better the body "stacks up" the more support it receives through the legs to the pelvis and the more energy it can utilize.

In standing and walking[3] there are two major planes of balance to be concerned with — front to back and side to side. In assessing side to side balance we are concerned with patterns of dexterity. If a carpenter drives nails all day with his right hand, his body will be over-developed on that side. This can create a great deal of discomfort over time as overworked muscles begin pulling the skeleton out of alignment. A postal carrier with a heavily weighted shoulder bag (carried mostly on the same side) has to contend with repetitive stresses and strains in the same areas of the body. Switching the bag from shoulder to shoulder may give some short term relief, but it will not alleviate the imbalanced patterns in the body which have been building for years. A basic understanding of body mechanics can really help in these situations. By changing the old patterns, stress can be released with more energy available for use in developing more efficient solutions to these constant demands.

Tension can be referred into areas of the body that aren't directly involved in a particular movement. For example, a carpenter will obviously put direct stress on the

1.   Even if you are not ready for the manipulation part of Rolfing you could still greatly benefit from working with a Rolfing Movement Teacher to find the most efficient position of use for your body at your work place.
2.   Of course the type of shoes we wear is of utmost importance in walking and standing. Consult the chapter "From The Ground Up" for information on shoes.
3.   For a concise account of human locomotion see "Walking: Focus on Motion" by James Tabor in Backpacker Magazine, pp. 40-49, April/May, 1981.

arm, shoulder girdle and portions of the mid and upper back on the hammering side. Referred tension may also go to the upper neck and head, creating symptoms seemingly unrelated to the work habits. Contruction workers constantly perform the actions of lifting, digging and carrying. Such jobs place a lot of stress on the lower back, buttocks, thighs, shoulders, upper back and arms. Again, the problem with referred tension is apparent as we see an over use of the neck[4] in lifting heavy objects. (Figures 49A,B)

It is possible to counter the imbalancing effects of one-sided work by using conscious awareness. One can begin by intentionally trying to do the less specialized work of lifting and carrying more on the "off side" and ensuring

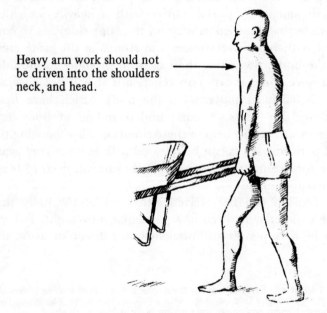

Heavy arm work should not
be driven into the shoulders
neck, and head.

FIGURE 49A

4.   See Chapter Eight on the shoulder girdle for more detail on this.

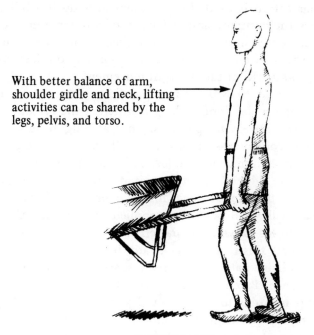

With better balance of arm, shoulder girdle and neck, lifting activities can be shared by the legs, pelvis, and torso.

FIGURE 49B

that the legs are able to push strongly when involved in any lifting action. This sounds simple, but it does illustrate what can be done by anyone whose work requires lifting, pulling, and pushing with one side more than the other. Studies[5] indicate that there is much less referred tension after Rolfing. In imbalanced bodies, repeated movements tend to compress and limit the free range of motion around joints. After Rolfing, joints are less compressed and able to move through a greater range of motion. As body parts return to balance a more effective pattern of

5.   Hunt, Valerie, "A Study of Structural Integration from Neuromuscular, Energy Field and Emotional Approaches," Dept. of Kinesiology, UCLA, 1977.

muscular action is used. Improvement in body flexibility increases the accuracy and efficiency of job performance. This also results in a decrease of accident and injury situations which often arise from poor coordination, lack of ability, and inefficient patterns of movement.

In addition to Rolfing manipulation, there are some things that can be done to help counteract the effects of imbalanced movement patterns. In watching others or looking at your own structure you will see a definite preference for standing on one leg. This causes the pelvis to adjust to the side, or to rotate as it attempts to center the weight over the support leg. This is a common pattern and one that will yield to some "applied awareness." Shift from leg to leg moving the pattern over to the unfamiliar side. At first this will feel awkward, but in time you will break this habit pattern and create space in your body for more balance. Parents always carry their children on the same hip in order to have their dexterous side free. Try carrying your child on your more dexterous hand whenever you can — your whole body will feel better and you will educate your less dexterous side.

All of the foregoing are related to side to side balance. When we add considerations of front-to-back balance the problems become more difficult to perceive. Taken together, these two planes of function will often set spirals of imbalance into the structure. (Figures 50A,B) This means that if a person carries their head forward of the ribcage and their pelvis tucked way under them and has a strong preference for using one side of their body, over time their structure will be twisted. The imbalance can run from one leg across the back and up the opposite side of the neck.

The front-to-back posture configurations are somewhat difficult to self-correct, but applied awareness and a "little help from your friend" (Rolfer) will go a long way toward easing a strong preference. Have someone take your picture in profile. Study this to see what you can work on.

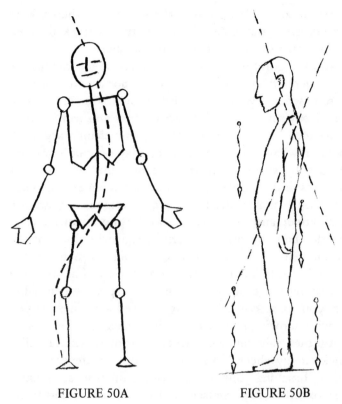

FIGURE 50A   FIGURE 50B

Long standing use patterns cause the body to adapt side to side and front to back.

Rolfers take pictures of their clients before and after they have received ten sessions of Rolfing. In their "before one" pictures, people are often amazed at the plainly visible imbalances in their bodies. After looking at your picture, see if you can "take up the slack" of your imbalance a little. Can you move your head and ribcage into a better relationship with your pelvis, legs, and feet, forming an imaginary vertical line to the ground? Don't strain to do this. Pay attention to how you can subtly create this alignment when you are walking down the street, or when you're working. Let your knees float and try to track parallel, don't attempt to force the feet into parallel.

Another good way to learn more about the imbalances and movement preferences in your body is to observe yourself when swimming. This provides a great non-stressed environment which reveals how you can improve the balance in your body. Doing the elementary back stroke, crawl and breast stroke, you may see that your arm pull may be stronger on one side and the movement of your arms and shoulder girdle may be asymmetrical. Your neck muscles may restrict the free movement of your arm and shoulder and your pelvis may be more restricted on one side than the other in various leg kicks. Your ankle-foot may also turn out on one side and turn in on the other side while kicking, and so on. Review your structure one region at a time. Allow one week per area initially. Then you may return for more focused awareness as you play with allowing new openness in your body.

Another valuable self awareness tool is what I call a "quick energy check." All you do is stop whatever you are doing — brushing your teeth, washing the dishes, writing a letter or more large muscle tasks such as moving furniture, lifting children and groceries or simply gripping a steering wheel — to see how you are doing these things. (Figure 51) The purpose of taking this "feeling picture" is to determine just how much effort (energy) is required to accomplish any given activity. No more or less than is necessary will do. Check yourself out, you'll be amazed at how much energy you can save if you release the un-natural patterns of holding. The best thing you can do is consult with a Rolfing Movement Teacher and let them help you become more aware of your movement patterns and how to improve them.

Many construction workers experience environmental and stress induced injuries and accidents. A client named

FIGURE 51
Take a "quick energy check". How does your body feel, where are you working too hard?

Hector worked for a dry wall company, putting up heavy sheet rock. Hector missed a lot of work because his knee or back was always going out, causing him to quit work until the injured area "healed."

"If I hadn't got so much improvement in my health from Rolfing I know my boss would have had to lay me off."

Hector's newly organized body allows him to carry the sheet rock in a more balanced and effective manner so that no one area is receiving more than its fair share of stress.

After Rolfing, Hector's Rolfing Movement Teacher went to his job site to observe his repetitive activities. She instructed him on how to use his body with greater awareness and efficiency. With a newly aligned body and new awareness of how to use his structure, Hector has not had to miss any days of work from structural related problems. His foreman was very impressed and has invited the Rolfing Movement Teacher back to work with some of his other employees.

EMOTIONAL STRESS

The body responds to stress by changing its shape in a number of ways. These shapes tell us something about what and how we have experienced our lives. Sometimes the body will thicken or thin out depending upon the specific type of stress. This thinning or thickening will influence the positioning of muscles and bones and change the shape and placement of organs leading to compression and twisting of the spine and changes in the shape and position of the diaphragm. This can cause a crowding of the cavities above (chest, heart, lungs) or below (abdomen, colon, kidneys, etc.) which then may alter the relative positions of the thorax, pelvis, or abdomen. This ultimately results in a change of the body's position in relation to the ideal line of gravity flowing through the body. Such changes eventually influence the way we think, feel, and act. In this way we can see the intricate and reciprocal relationship between structure and function or how body shape influences body feeling and how body feelings shape body structure. Once we understand these relationships we can use this information to develop guidelines for how we organize and use our structures.

"A *person* may lie to you, but the *body* does not lie!" Ida Rolf discussed this idea many times in her classes. She meant that we can conceal things mentally but by "reading" the body we get a more accurate view of a person's true mental/emotional state. Rolfers are interested in how the body is used to express, withhold, confuse, cover up, release, or lock in the emotional states and long standing character patterns of the person. Our personal life story is recorded in the flesh and revealed through the outward form of body structure. Any long standing structural distortion carries with it or is supported by a corresponding mental/emotional set. To the trained observer, body shape tells *what* we have experienced in our life and *how* we have experienced it. It tells whether we have been *masters* or *victims* of our lives.

Of course the overall body pattern is a composite record which includes genetic input, societal and family influences, as well as the more current stresses of life — habitual attitudes and emotional issues expressed and repressed. The point to understand here is that all of these influences create compensations and imbalances in body structure and function. From this information we are able to understand that a structurally based system of logical evaluation can be used to explain the cause/effect relationships between the nature of our feeling life and the shape of our bodies.

From my years of observation it seems that hardly anyone fits neatly into any of the somato-typing systems of Reich, Lowen, Keleman, Kurtz and the rest. Rather, I have found that most are combinations of the basic categories. Nonetheless, correlations can be found between the basic somatic shapes and the forms of behavioral expression they employ.

These combination or hybrid types are reflected in the body through systems of structural holding and compensation which are in effect physical expressions of mental/emotional imbalance in the person. They can be likened to "mixed emotional messages" which take root in the flesh.

One of the basic goals of Rolfing involves unwinding structural compensations and re-establishing a state of congruence in the body. This congruence or level of corresponding harmony includes the many basic *structural* goals of Rolfing such as balancing the body front to back, side to side, surface to deep,[6] etc., but moreover it includes *energetic* and *functional* qualities of balance and harmony in the body-person. This is where a basic understanding of the general body habitus of any person becomes valuable. We would then begin to assess the general hybrid body type of the person and the degree of congruence between the top and bottom halves of the body from structural, energetic and functional perspectives. The *energetic* evaluation includes the quality and quantity of the breathing pattern, as well as the fluid (blood, lymph, etc.) flow throughout the structure. This information indicates how we interact with others. This also includes the quality of the digestive flows, indicating how we take in, "assimilate" and "eliminate" physically and emotionally. This also includes the degree of muscle tonus from one area to another, which can be simply classified as *over-bound* or *under-bound*. And the degree to which internal feeling in the body has been altered would also be an energetic evalua-' tion. From this we could determine if the person is too *porous* (emotions overflow) and ungrounded or if they are too *dense* (emotions dammed up) and dogmatically *rigid.*[7] *Functional* considerations focus upon movement patterns, joint immobility or hypermobility, weight bearing imbalances, and basic mechanical considerations of how we interact with the gravity field. It would also give us infor-

6.   See Chapter 1, pages 1 and 2 for a discussion of the general structural goals of Rolfing.
7.   This presentation of somato-psychic body patterns is not intended to be conclusive in any way. These categories of over/under bound, porous, dense, and rigid, etc. will give you some general idea about the ways people use the body to dramatize character.

mation about whether the person basically moves *away* from, *towards*, or *against* the people in his world.

All three of these body evaluations — structural, energetic and functional — give us a composite "print out" of the nature of the person's *emotional life*. We can further differentiate between constitutional and acute stages of bodily imbalance. The constitutional body pattern includes genetic inheritance and the impacts of long-standing life-shaping events such as the birth experience, major accidents, surgeries or mental/physical insults and assaults. The acute body pattern represents the individual's more current personal history or recent injuries. A person may come for body-work showing a hostile, puffed up, over-bounded and aggressive body style. This may be the result of a current emotional stress. Once this acute manifestation has been resolved we may find that underneath is a collapsed/resigned and fearful pattern which is the true constitution of the person. The acute must usually be resolved before lasting changes can be brought about in the constitutional.

Regardless of the pattern, the basic goal becomes one of unwinding the structural imbalances and compensations and re-establishing a state of congruence. Knowledge of a person's structural, energetic and functional imbalances allows the Rolfer an opportunity to plan a more individualized strategy to employ during a basic 10 hour cycle of Rolfing sessions. As each body has a different "lock up" system, the more specific information we have to arrive at the right "combination" for unlocking the body pattern and allowing it to return to a healthy state, the easier it is to accomplish our goals. This sort of individualized approach allows for more specific structural changes which give the client sensorial feedback about the relationship between structural order and healthy mental/emotional functioning. If there are significant mental/emotional imbalances which do not resolve themselves during

.the course of a person's Rolfing I then refer the client to one of my colleagues in the psychological community who is better equipped to help the client find effective solutions for their condition.

The following case history will give you an appreciation of what I mean when I refer to hybrid body types and will also illustrate structural, functional and energetic congruence/incongruence. Sheila (not her real name) came to be Rolfed when she had her 32nd birthday. She felt this was "about time to make some significant changes in my life." She complained of low back pain (structural), recurring temporal headaches (a combination pattern), low energy (energetic) and "a right knee that gives out when I climb stairs" (functional). "For once I would like to change my pear body", (pointing to her hips, buttocks and upper thighs) "into a shape I can be proud of." Looking at Sheila's pictures we observed structural, energetic and functional incongruence, especially between the top and bottom halves of the body. Her hips, pelvis and upper thighs were indeed very heavy and dense while her upper body appeared quite small and restricted. The two body halves just didn't seem to match. The conflict or incongruence in her mental/emotional make-up began to reveal itself around session five which focuses upon the diaphragm and abdomen, chest, shoulders and arms. Sheila began feeling very angry, almost hostile toward her boss, specifically, and generally irritated with most men. She realized that most of her life she had tried to be nice to men but at the same time she often felt resentful and that most men tried to take advantage of the reserved and gentle nature which she presented to the world.[8] As the Rolfing sessions progressed we noticed that the lower half

---

8.　It should be pointed out that Sheila's father deserted her family when Sheila was 7. Her mother and two older sisters took care of their household until Sheila left home for college at 18.

of Sheila's body was the receptacle for her anger, but the upper half of the body was so shy and stilled that the energetic activity necessary to express her true feelings never circulated up to the chest, arms and throat, (her means of expressing these feelings). One of our mutually agreed upon goals became the healthy release, expression and management of the feelings and behaviors associated with this incongruent pattern. As we had hoped, when Sheila's body incongruence pattern began to release we also observed and were overjoyed by a corresponding resolution of her incongruent mental/emotional pattern. Sheila was able to contact, understand, release and harmonize the incongruent mental/emotional states reflected by her body structure. She became aware of the primary source of her anger and found effective outlets for its release and resolution through a new routine of physical activity and new found confidence in addressing those people whom she felt offended by. Freud was accurate when he suggested that "anatomy is destiny". Body structure does indeed "shape" feeling and emotional expression. Sheila noted, "as the pear gets smaller" (lower body) "my upper body gets fuller. My energy seems to be back and it sure is easier for me to express my true feelings without guilt."

Emotional stresses enter the body along existing lines of strain. (Stresses always do the most damage in the weakest link of a system.) Over time, the body gets held in a contracted state, unable to relax. Constant thinking, anxiety and internal chatter will cause neurological and muscular contractions that remain in the body. The body never really rests. This interferes with the normal rhythms of charge and discharge, expansion and contraction. A cyclical release and buildup of tension that occurs naturally in the body to maintain equilibrium will be disrupted.

Stewart is fifty-three years old and has been a successful psychotherapist for sixteen years. He has been reading about and considering the possibility of being Rolfed for nearly six years. Stewart sits slouched over in a chair all day, listening to people discuss their personal problems. When he stands up, his upper body still appears as if it is slouched in a chair. His chin and throat almost touch his chest and his shoulders hunch way forward.

"After listening to others' problems for so long I began to have trouble sorting out my own emotions from those I think my clients are struggling with. My body feels more like a time bomb waiting for someone to please pull the pin so I can release some of this pressure. From my Rolfing I've just begun to realize that I have a body and the joy that being at peace within my body brings."

As we age it seems that we get stuck more and more on the contraction side of the equation. Becoming more "civilized" has caused us to lose our natural abilities for balancing charge and discharge. Older workers often become less efficient at their jobs because of the cumulative effects of mental stress and the use of improper muscular patterns. Rolfing could help to improve some of the structural factors commonly attributed to just "getting old." Improved order in the body could help workers of all ages to become more efficient, productive, creative and happier in the professions they choose.

Ray came to Rolfing at the age of fifty-seven. Still eight years short of retirement he found his job to be a more and more stressful and demoralizing experience. The quality and quantity of his work had been continually decreasing over the last five years.

"I hate to go to work anymore. I feel useless there. I'd quit tomorrow if I didn't need that damn pension."

Ray's body showed what years of stress, repetitive movements and imbalance in body structure can do to one's alignment. His body really looked beat, which is the way Ray said he felt. His structure was losing and gravity was winning. After Rolfing, Ray made a complete turnaround. His newly balanced body gave him increased energy and improvement in his job followed. This made him feel better about himself and the respect of his co-workers began to reappear. It is almost never too late to provide some degree of help to those open to the possibility of improvement.

I have seen that Rolfed bodies accumulate less tension. This improves their ability to maintain a balanced state as fewer drastic mood swings will occur. A Rolfed body more naturally balances physical and mental stresses. This serves as positive feedback, further reinforcing the desire to do well.

In addition to re-balancing bodies that do the work, principles from Rolfing can be applied to improve the design and efficiency of the work environment itself. Furniture, tools, clothing, lighting and equipment could be designed to support efficient and effective use of body structure while minimizing the effects of gravitational stress. We have already seen how car seats could be altered to support balanced body structure. We have also observed the most efficient relationship of a seated worker to his work. It is not within the scope of this work to detail the changes in furniture and equipment that could be made, but the following should give some seed ideas.

Most living room furniture should be designed to support the lower back more completely and to allow the height of the pelvis to be just above the knee. Kitchen chairs should have a slight forward tilt at the seat to allow the organs of digestion to be relaxed and completely supported by the pelvis. The height and seat angle of most toilet seats does not support efficient lower bowel functioning (the knees are too low). The height of most sinks (bathroom and kitchen) and counter tops increases strain and tension in the lower back and neck areas. Most office and business furniture (desks, chairs, tables) and equipment (typewriters, computers, cash registers) could be redesigned with Rolfing principles in mind. The quality and volume of work being performed by balanced bodies in a supportive environment would surely improve.

At rest, work, or play, Rolfing principles can be applied to improve how we expend our energy. By removing structural imbalances, we open the way for a better level of functioning in whatever we do.

11

BODY PLAY

Many years ago, in a Sunday supplement, I saw a picture of the Olympic races. Among the first three or four contestants in this picture, the thing that was so outstanding was that the man who won was operating in form and all of the others were operating out of desperation that they had to get there. The front runner was perfectly quiet and easy and could have carried on a conversation all the time he was running. This is form.

I.P.R.

An exciting part of being a Rolfer is seeing how significantly people's lives begin changing as their bodies change. When people feel their bodies improving they want to carry this spirit of improvement over into other aspects of their lives. The changes in their lifestyle might include a healthier diet, new regularity in sleep and rest patterns, starting a new exercise program, beginning a new sport or dance and incorporating a system of relaxation or meditation into their routine. As new levels of balance are experienced in the body, balance becomes a key goal in other dimensions of life. The next two chapters focus upon two areas of lifestyle change — exercise and diet.

There has been increased interest in all forms of sport, exercise and dance in the last few years. More and more Americans are participating in jogging, tennis, racquetball, swimming and other types of exercise. Performance and

enjoyment of these activities can be increased by understanding the Rolfing point of view. When selecting your
activities find a form of physical exercise suited for your
body structure and personality type. This activity should
be integrated into your other routines and viewed with as
much importance as eating and sleeping. Crash programs
do not have long lasting effects. A short-term commitment
remains just that — short lived and non-transformative.
A change in lifestyle must be made to integrate the activities into your daily routine.

Different body types are suited for specific activities.
If you are compact and heavy boned, the repetitive, compressive movements of long distance running are probably
not for you. If you are frail and have brittle bones, then
contact sports probably will do you more harm than good.
Balance is once again the key when considering activities
appropriate to your personality. For example, if you have
a very sedentary job and you happen to be the type of
person who "holds on" to their emotions, activities involving expressive movements, such as dance, karate, and
racquetball would be useful. Remember that you need a
balance between charge and discharge — the taking in and
releasing of energy — to maintain health. If you're not a
morning person, don't decide with the best intentions that
you'll get up each morning at five thirty to run before you
go to work. "I don't have time to exercise" is the most
common excuse given. Unless you work more than 10
hours a day, five days a week, you can find time for a
regular exercise program. It becomes a matter of priority.
If health, enjoyment and balance are not included in your
values then the likelihood of continuing an exercise program is very faint. If time and interest permit, I encourage
you to become involved in more than one activity. Keep in
mind the need for balance between the various components of fitness such as strength, agility, flexibility, cardiovascular efficiency and most important of all — the mean-

ingfulness of the activity.

Let's use an example to give a better idea of how to select activities which are appropriate for character and body structure. Kevin is 5'9", 160 lbs., with a dense skeleton and well-defined musculature. By his own admission he has a tendency to not express his feelings very easily. He is very intelligent and has received most of his "strokes" through intellectual achievement. Halfway through his sixth session of Rolfing he began asking questions about diet and exercise. He wanted exercise to enhance his health and to help towards preventing future problems. In addition, Kevin wanted to exercise for stress release and to participate in competitive activities. He decided to try running and racquetball. He wanted to become good at road running so he could join many of his friends who already enjoyed this sport. He even dreamed of training for a marathon. I strongly discouraged him from pursuing this goal because it would create compression and wear and tear on his already stocky frame. We compromised and he said he would focus on races up to twelve miles. Kevin realized that it was going to take a long time for him to run even four miles, so we decided to set short term, feasible goals that were sure to be realized. So many people, enthused by watching runners in their area or the New York marathon on T.V., start to train with real enthusiasm. Within a week, 95 percent of these idealists have quit. Setting realistic goals is a must in changing your lifestyle. It's too easy to get discouraged and quit if careful planning is not coupled with initial enthusiasm.

Because Kevin had been sedentary for so long, we followed the advice outlined by Kenneth Cooper and other aerobic specialists and started with a walking program followed by stress testing and the development of a running schedule.[1] In addition, we focused on the time of day best

---

1.   See Kenneth Cooper, M.D., *The New Aerobics*, Bantam Books, 1979.

suited for Kevin's work schedule, biorhythms, and temperament, as well as a balance between running alone for serenity and self confidence and training with other runners for companionship and encouragement. He also varied the environment and terrain that he ran on — hills, flat surfaces, and desert mesa — to reduce boredom and to exercise different parts of his body. All of this had to be balanced with his other activity choice — racquetball.

"I want to get fairly good in racquetball, but I don't care about playing in tournaments. Mostly I want to use it as a way to let off steam and allow my anger to come out by smashing the hell out of that little ball."

Again, Kevin set realistic goals for himself, took lessons and warmed up before playing. Six months later, Kevin began to feel the need for more flexibility. The running had created some shortening in his body, so stretching seemed the best remedy. He enrolled in a yoga and meditation class at the community college. These activities helped increase his flexibility and made him feel more calm and relaxed. With this program and his newly Rolfed body, Kevin is on his way to a healthy lifestyle.

American schooling has emphasized physical training for children and teens. However, there is a new wave of exercise programs for adults and senior citizens. Many people join these programs and undertake a new physical activity without giving sufficient attention as to whether it is appropriate for their body or temperament. A person beginning a new physical activity shouldn't consider it a fad to try out, but a nourishing physical challenge that will raise the quality of his or her life. It has been said "You don't stop playing because you're old. You grow old because you stop playing." Enjoyable, meaningful activity is an essential part of life. People are most likely to continue an activity over a lifetime if it is fun and challenging, as well as merely "good for them." Kenneth Cooper, M.D., founder of the Acrobic Center in Dallas, Texas, notes "There's a saying that when a person dies, he dies not so much from disease as from his entire life."[2]

In light of this, it is important to distinguish between the "appearance" of health and the "experience" of health. As a society we have accepted advertising's visual aesthetic, primarily derived from athletes and fashion models. This image supposedly represents the "healthy body." The focus is on what health looks like and not what health feels like. Many health clubs, fitness clubs, figure salons and the like sell programs by getting people concerned with how they look. The consumer is supposed to fit his or her body to a popular image. Without exactly explaining how, the ads imply that "if your body looks this way (Figures 52A,B) you will automatically feel better." I urge cautious evaluation of all these advertised programs of health and fitness which focus on the appearance of health.

The "look" adopted by most girls and women includes elements from the "Playboy" image and high fashion modeling, as well as from athletics. In this model, we often see the chest pulled up high in the front, which causes the shoulder blades to be pulled together and the spine to sit more deeply forward in the body than normal. This pattern also compresses the ribs and keeps them from moving through their full range. The flat, hard stomach and narrow waist that goes with this form flexes the diaphragm and restricts breathing. The buttocks are held tightly and pulled inward, causing adjustment in the legs and reducing responsiveness in the pelvis. Everyone who tries to force themselves into these unnatural forms ends up creating an imbalance and unnecessary stress in their bodies.

Cheryl was a fashion model who spent a great deal of

2.   Vogue, October 1981, "New Frontiers of Fitness" by Janice Kaplan, pp. 515-519.

FIGURE 52A

FIGURE 52B

her life trying to fit her body to the image we have been discussing. She had a pulled up chest, pinched in waist and very round buttocks. She even went so far as to have cosmetic surgery on her breasts, as the agency said they were sagging too much for the image they wanted to convey. When Cheryl came to be Rolfed she complained mostly of low back pain, a stiff neck, headaches, low energy and a "nagging pain in my breastbone that shoots straight through to my back." Initially she felt very uneasy as her body began to relax and return to its natural form. "It's hard to educate yourself in letting go when you've spent so much time holding on," she said. After a few sessions, the new sensations of ease and comfort began to be welcomed and she knew she was on the right track. She became aware of how much she had allowed others to dictate how she should be.

"Now that I'm not trying to hold my chest and shoulders up, the shooting pains have stopped and for once I don't have a headache. I feel like a fool for allowing myself to be conned by such superficial ideas."

Cheryl used to almost starve herself to maintain her figure. She now eats a more balanced diet and does belly dance and plays tennis to release tension and "keep the weight off." The lure of the "image" is seductive and persuasive. We must be careful not to get trapped into pursuing goals that end up reducing our health and perpetuating stereotyped images of who we are and how we should look.

From the Rolfing perspective, a preoccupation with external form is a misplaced priority and especially so when the body's internal processes are not functioning well. Criteria for a healthy body should go beyond the mere improvement of strength, muscle development, and external appearance. A well-organized body insures healthy functioning — good digestion and elimination, clear skin, normal blood pressure and all processes which provide the person with adequate emotional and physical resources. If activities are chosen only for cosmetic value, the ability to create a healthy, functioning body will be limited. A good looking body is a by-product of activity, rather than the object of the exercise. Selection of physical activities which internally nourish and ensure a positive experience are critical.

So what does "internally nourishing" movement feel like? Such an experience is difficult to describe. The saying "one person's pleasure is another person's pain" is true. The right experience is different for each person, but if you trust your internal perceptions, you will "know it" when you find the activity that is right for you. Internally nourishing movement feels right from the inside, complements body structure and personality (i.e. it supports balance and body usage patterns and emotional expressiveness), allows for a balanced charge and discharge of the body's energy, promotes healthy self-confidence through mastery of the activity, is enjoyable, and makes one want to repeat the activity regularly. It culminates in an intuitive sense that "this is the right activity for me."

Meaningful activity focuses on the experience of the whole body, rather than on the results and overdevelopment of individual body parts. The "results" approach would be exemplified by the "body builder" who decides to tone up his abdominal musculature, or enlarge the diameter of his neck to balance it with his shoulders. These piecemeal approaches do not create an integrated structure. In a balanced body, resistance exercises can be used to increase strength, as long as one area doesn't get significantly overdeveloped than another.

Internally nourishing movement allows the whole person to become enveloped in the activity. At such moments we are able to suspend our judgements, lose the fears, inhibitions and insecurities which fill so much of our time.

". . . It (nourishing movement) is characterized by an inner sense of passionate appreciation for the unique insights that you can discover from the body."[3] This transforming movement offers opportunities to experience unity, inner strength, personal fulfillment and a sense of physical maturity.

Rolfing is concerned with exploring the components involved in the experience of integration. Meaningful movement is one aspect in an integrated experience. Integration also includes physical grace, a balance between strength and flexibility and a balance in the action of deep muscles and their counterparts nearer the body surface. Integration ensures efficient use of energy and enhanced physical performance. Physiological integration, as previously discussed, would include an increase in fluid circulation and high level functioning of all organ systems. At the emotional and psychological levels, we would expect to see qualities of resilience and adaptability. This means a quick recovery from emotional disappointments, with minimal fear and anxiety patterns[4] and relative freedom from one's past, i.e. living in the present and not letting past episodes (traumas, etc.) override your current experience of life.

Beth, a woman who had been receiving Rolfing sessions for almost two years for injuries suffered during a serious car accident, was taking Tai Chi for nearly six years when she just happened to play racquetball with a friend.

"I knew almost immediately that although I love the movement of Tai Chi, it was reinforcing my tendency to be quiet and shy. Racquetball provides the aggressive, competitive activity I need to discharge all my pent-up energy

3.   Allen and Fahey, *Being Human in Sport*, Lea and Febiger, Philadelphia, 1977, pp. 111-12.
4.   For an enlightening discussion of fear and the body, see *Faces of Fear* by Hugh Lynn Cayce, Harper and Row, S.F., 1980.

and emotions. I never thought I'd enjoy chasing a little blue ball around, but it sure has been good for me."

Often the undertaking of new activities will challenge the capacity of the heart and lungs. This may be uncomfortable initially and is often enough to discourage further involvement. To avoid over-taxing your breathing and heart rate too soon, your approach to exercise should be progressive and gentle. You don't have to suffer to get fit. Duration can be substituted for intensity. Run slowly for a longer period of time. In the search for a meaningful activity, the starting point may be as simple as taking a brisk walk every day. As the capacity of the body increases, more demand can be placed on it. Once the body can tolerate certain demands without undue pain, then specific sports or activities can be safely explored and more clearly evaluated.

In this society, it seems we are mostly concerned with and rewarded for accomplishments in specialized skill areas — often at the expense of a more balanced sense of self. The way to "get ahead" in business seems to become more efficient and highly specialized, but increasingly confined within narrow limits. The same "thinking" seems to be carrying over to physical activity. Now more than ever, parents are encouraging young children to specialize in a particular sport, hoping to produce superstars. This tendency has carried over to the general population in their choice of sporting activities. Perhaps the following example will help to illustrate this point. Mike is an outstanding amateur racquetball player. He plays in many tournaments and practices 3 to 4 hours every day. Racquetball is not only his sport, it seems to be his life. Mike's eyes are set deep in the sockets, slightly sad and questioning. His skin is pale and his overall movement style is restricted and seemingly calculated, as are his words. When asked how he is doing, he always says "good" and then proceeds to talk about his racquetball game. He defines his state of being by the ups and downs of his skill. Mike's body is tense and tight. In a close match it appears that he may explode at any moment. He plays no other sport beside racquetball and seems to have no other interests. He finds it difficult to relax after a match. Returning to a state of equilibrium is nearly impossible because tension is the constant fuel for Mike's movement. Mike is a victim of overspecialization — focusing on one skill at the expense of more comprehensive development. He truly excels in his chosen activity, but his drive for perfection interferes with other areas of his life. He lacks close friends, marriages have not worked and he can't hold a job. His attitude toward himself and life in general is too narrow. His obsession with racquetball has made him less skilled and flexible in dealing with other aspects of his life. Mike could benefit from Rolfing principles and by selecting movement activities appropriate to his body and temperament. Directing his attention away from performance and external form toward health and meaning would create more balance in his body and life. He might even be able to play racquetball for enjoyment.

This overspecialization can also lead to structural problems where, as previously discussed, the stronger already healthy areas get overworked and the weaker, less healthy body regions remain unattended. This overspecialization perpetuates musculo-skeletal imbalances, increases long term deterioration and overall shortens the quality and quantity of one's life.

Tony has been running competitively since he was on the cross country team in high school. A successful middle distance runner in college, he has continued his love of running by competing in amateur races. Now at the age of thirty-four he has begun to suffer from shin splints, heel bruises, painful knees and numbness in his right foot. His body has used up its ability to adapt to the repetitive and cumulative stresses that running more than thirty-five miles a week eventually causes most people. Tony's upper body looks fairly young and trim, but his pelvis, legs and feet look worn out. He still wants to continue running, but his imbalanced structure is making it harder and harder for him to maintain the training schedule he used even last year.

"I feel like my will is the only thing keeping me going. My body doesn't love running anymore. But, for some reason, I still want to compete. I'm not sure what I'm trying to prove, but I train regularly and keep entering races.

Both Tony and Mike could benefit from a re-evaluation of their commitments to these activities and perhaps come to a compromise position which allows them to enjoy their sports while not seeing their bodies deteriorate so fast. Perhaps they could substitute some activities which are innately nourishing and which would not cause so much stress and imbalance.

People of all ages, shapes and sizes are taking to the streets, running tracks and jogging paths in record numbers. Running magazines, camps and workshops devoted to running, corporate sponsorship of races and the influence of running wear upon the fashion industry all reflect the ever expanding impact of the running/jogging craze. As the new legion of "weekend" athletes push their bodies to the limit, there has been a corresponding increase in stresses, sprains, dislocations, shin splints, and other injuries. This has created a newly expanding field of specialization — "sports medicine." Many sport-related injuries are caused by poor structure. For example, imbalance of the leg muscles, no matter how it comes about, will determine how the legs are used in movement. Improper movement patterns increase the possibility of injury. Many competitive runners and casual joggers complain of lower back pain, stiffness, and sore hip joints. The causes of such pain are numerous. But one factor most running advisors and specialists in exercise fail to consider is the overall structural balance of the body. The body is the vehicle by which all movement activities are accomplished and enjoyed. It follows that the better organized our "equipment" is, the better we will perform. Rolfing balances the body so that running related injuries such as shin splints, achilles tendon strains, and hamstring pulls can be minimized, if not totally avoided. I do not feel that running is ·inherently bad. However, most bodies are not adequately organized to handle the compression and long term wear and tear that running places on the body. Experience indicates that only a small percentage of the population should run more than four daily miles, four to five times a week. Experts agree that at most, 10 to 15 percent of people are naturally built for running. I recommend that you leave the long distance running to those endowed with the type of body capable of handling such specific stresses and strains. It seems that the body type best suited for long distances is relatively long-boned with a naturally low percentage of body fat and a highly efficient metabolic process. I call this type the "greyhound." This is the kind of person who tends to stay slim no matter what they eat and regardless of whether they exercise. If you do decide to run, whether your body type is suited for it or not, go get Rolfed so that you are running with the most balanced structure possible for you.

From the standpoint of all components of integration I feel that walking is generally more appropriate and suitable to a wider range of body types than long distance running. A person can derive much joy and sufficient physiological benefit from a systematic program of vigorous walking. It is safe, easy and requires no equipment other than a pair of comfortable, well-made shoes. Walking can be done alone (it is a great relaxer), in couples (a nice way to get to know someone) or in activity groups (for companionship and community spirit). Walking is basically risk-free and, unlike jogging, it is almost impossible to walk too much. Walking can act as a stimulant or a tranquilizer. There are no age limitations, and it does increase our level of fitness as it burns calories and tones up the body. The human body is naturally designed for walking. Allow walking to become a habit in your life, until it becomes as important as eating and sleeping.[5] Beatrice is ninety-one years of age. She was first Rolfed at the age of eighty-two. Her body is in excellent condition. She is a lifetime walker.

"I try to walk at least one mile a day, no matter what. On those rare days when weather keeps me inside I'll ride my exercycle, but it's not any fun. I love to be outdoors, feel the earth under me and let my thoughts just wander."

The rage to belong to a health club still seems to be continuing throughout the 80's. Most of the men and women who exercise seem to be focusing on "getting in shape" through some cardiovascular activity and gaining "strength" through some form of weight training. When I go to one of these clubs I see men and women in their 30's, 40's and 50's trying to do the same workouts and mold their bodies into the same form as the 18-25 year olds. Perhaps the most important consideration in designing an exercise program is having realistic body image expectations that are congruent with one's stage of development. This implies shaping a body style by selecting acti-

5.   For more information on walking, see *The Wonderful World of Walking*, Bill Gale, Delta Books, 1981.

vities consistent with creating length, alignment, balance, flexibility, a free exchange of fluids and pressures and which "balance out" the temperament extremes of the individual. These are the foundational goals of a lifestyle/ fitness program that you can follow and benefit from over the span of a lifetime. This is not the kind of imagery and expectations created for us by the advertising and health promotion industries. We must create our own based on what is inherently good for the structural well-being and longevity of the physical body. I call this a form of body maturity which basically means knowing the "what," "when," and "how" of organizing and nourishing the physical structure with exercise. The "what" refers mostly to one's visual aesthetic. One should ask "towards what visual image am I moving, what mental picture do I have of what I want my body to look like as a result of my physical training program?" The "when" refers to timing. Is my desired image consistent with where I am in life's journey chronologically? If I am 45 is my image generally consistent with the glandular, metabolic and structural realities of my age? Or am I trying to force my physical body into a form which is inconsistent with its "blueprint?" The "how" refers to selection of appropriate activities to accomplish one's goals. One should ask "Am I balancing my activity selections to ensure that the components of fitness most essential to my stage of development are being covered?" For example, as we age we usually lose flexibility, circulation, cardiovascular efficiency and strength in this order. It would then follow that lifting weights should not be the focus of our program at the age of 35 and beyond. This means activity selection which covers the appropriate component of fitness and which provides a balancing element to our basic character structure. For example, if one is a hard-driving, intense kind of person (the classic type A personality that is most likely to have cardio-vascular problems), it might behoove them to try some activities which allow the system to slow down, gently release tension and quiet the "chattering mind." Unfortunately such a person is more likely to focus on strength building with weight training, which would tend to develop more muscular tightening while "locking in" even more securely the extremes of their personality type and the stress patterns that are created by this particular personal style. Once again, this type of exercise tends to place extra stress on an already unbalanced body. The net result is that the imbalances are increased and the already healthy body parts get still more healthy and the weak body systems are less able to cope with the increased discrepancy in balance. The final outcome is a body less capable of dealing with stress over the long term. In other words, only the muscular areas that are free to receive the various benefits of exercise will benefit, while those areas which are undernourished, overbound and loaded with degenerated tissue (feels like "gristle" or a "walnut" when you touch it) will not receive any lasting benefits from this exercise. So the wrong exercise selection simply serves to perpetuate and in fact increases muscular imbalances and asymmetries and locks in existing patterns of tension.

If stress is a response pattern that is continued over time and becomes part of the structure, then the activities that a person chooses (supposedly to reduce stress) should not distort the body and further reinforce the stress pattern. In the example being used, weight training would continue to add internal pressure to the system, tighten the muscles most desperately in need of length and greater pliability, and reinforce the person's feelings of needing to push themselves, to force and hold onto everything from their money to their breathing with the same degree of intensity. This creates a body-self running on false energy, driven by the needs of the ego. Choosing weight training as the focal point of an exercise program will further imprison this person in a body pattern heading for self destruction.

With a healthy shift in body-image expectations and self-perception, this person could move toward balance by selecting some activity such as racquetball which is still an outlet for their competitive nature. Racquetball, unlike the weight workouts, would allow a healthy expression of anger and release of its accompanying tension while ensuring a challenge to the cardiovascular system in such a manner that built-up pressure is released rather than increased. Such an activity selection could be the start of easing the temperament extremes from this person's disposition so that balance could also be achieved in other aspects of the person's life. So instead of using the body to control, hold back, lock in, and prevent outside interference and contact, it could learn to be used as the vehicle which reaches out to engage others, satisfies internal needs and desires, increases empathetic feelings, and gives hope for the future. The choice is ours to make. We must first understand the behavioral relationship between anatomy, the shape of our structure and feeling, and the internal sensations and states created by the form of our bodies.

Many people involved in sport are concerned with developing more body strength to improve their movement performance.[6] From a Rolfing perspective, the components of strength include balance, proper positioning of muscle groups and an increased range of joint motion. On the level of mechanics, the balance is between complimentary groups of muscles, such as the biceps and triceps of the upper arm. For example, in normal movement, the triceps will begin extending (lengthen) as the biceps flex (shorten). If these muscles are appropriately balanced,

---

6. You must remember that regardless of specific claims, resistance exercise will shorten fibers and contract connective tissue. If you choose such exercise, I strongly encourage you to allocate a corresponding amount of time for lengthening and stretching activities to counterbalance the compressive effects of resistance exercise.

movement can have a vigorous, forceful quality even though less effort is expended. This natural relationship is disrupted when the body becomes too bulky with overly contracted muscles. Most coaches, athletic trainers and physicians giving exercise advice tend to focus on developing the extrinsic or surface muscles. I have found that over-developed, bulging muscles tend to contract the entire body.[7] This is another example of over development of particular body areas. What is suggested is that the development of too much bulk interferes with normal mechanical and physiological movements and the net result is as actual loss of muscle length, strength, mobility, resilience and efficiency. If the body is properly balanced with symmetrical distribution of fiber length and resiliency in all layers of the body, movement can be initiated from the deeper (intrinsic) muscles and continued by the extrinsics to a smooth completion. (Figures 53 and 54) This creates a wave-like motion of coordinated muscular action with less energy expended. In this way, the extrinsics (surface muscles) aren't over compensating for a lack of movement in the deeper muscles of the body (intrinsics). Consider the movement involved in throwing, common to such sports as baseball, football, the serve and overhead motion in tennis, the ceiling shot in racquetball, spiking in volleyball, and numerous others. If done improperly, or with imbalanced sets of muscles, throwing can place a great deal of strain upon the shoulder and arm, often referring

7.   "In most exercise, the exterior surface or extrinsic muscles just become bigger . . . Now when you have distended, hard, overexercised muscles, they are no longer capable of contracting and expanding, or relaxing. The tissue has been stretched to the point where it receives about as much contained fluid as it can handle and then it is apparently no longer able to contract, to force the fluid in. Flow of fluids will bring greater oxygen content to the muscles. When muscle is all engorged with fluid, it can't receive the interchange from the bloodstream that it needs to have enough oxygen present or to remove waste products." From *Ida Rolf Talks About Rolfing and Physical Reality*, Rosemary Feitis, Harper and Row, 1978, pp 49-50.

tensions[8] to the neck and upper back. The common complaints of shoulder and elbow bursitis are often a result of this type of misuse. After Rolfing, a more efficient throwing pattern will be created when the chest (pectoralis major) and back (teres and latissimus) muscles are in balance.

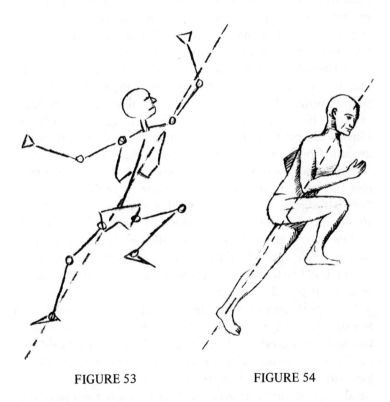

FIGURE 53   FIGURE 54

Using intrinsic muscles allows the body to lenthen during exertion with less energy expenditure.

8.   Referred tension – transfer of muscular effort and strain to other body parts seemingly not involved in the movement performed.

Rolfing baseball pitchers and football quarterbacks would improve their throwing pattern. A key question for them to consider would be "How efficiently is work (muscular action) being transmitted through my entire structure?" Instead of being so narrowly concerned with the size of the arm, the speed of release, and the strength of shoulder and upper back muscles, attention would also be paid to how well the feet are employed in generating power and effectively transmitting it through the body. How responsive are the ankle, knee and hip hinges in creating a continuous flow of movement in throwing actions?

Remember our discussion of the core/sleeve in which the movements of the periscope became restricted by its tight casing. Mike, the racquetball player, has overdeveloped his extrinsic muscles, his "casing." This causes him to use more energy just to move around. His intrinsics are not functioning — they are on "hold." To compensate for this lack of inner-outer balance, he does more exercise to pump up his extrinsics because he feels the need to "get stronger." Unfortunately, this approach only serves to compound the problem; the intrinsics become more locked in and the extrinsics are called upon to work even harder. Mike could benefit from some input about how to better use his body in such a way that the outer muscles would not get all the work.

The performance of athletes at all skill levels could be significantly improved if their bodies were structurally balanced. Studies[9] show that after Rolfing the body assumes visible postural changes, demonstrates more flexible and balanced movement and improved health. Structural organization removes imbalanced movement patterns and reduces the possibility of injury. More exhaustive

9.   Valerie V. Hunt, "A Study of Structural Integration from Neuromuscular, Energy Field, and Emotional Approaches," UCLA, 1977.

studies are needed to fully measure the effects of Rolfing in preventing injuries, and in speeding the rehabilitation process after injury. Rolfing clients report, however, that Rolfing makes a significant contribution in reducing sport-related injuries.

Thus far we have focused on improving performance by reorganizing physical structure. Body structure can contribute to the amount of anxiety a person has and can affect their performance.[10] Years of experience with clients shows that pent-up emotions are often released as chronically contracted muscles are loosened. This emotional discharge decreases the level of anxiety. A body that is structurally balanced and relatively free from anxiety will perform better. These principles are gradually finding their way into such areas as sport performance, athletic training methods, sports medicine, injury reduction, movement efficiency and other aspects of physical training.[11] In the very near future, we should see professional and college athletic teams employing Rolfers. The Rolfer would act as a consultant to sports teams, providing a unique perspective. Along with team trainers, conditioning experts, physicians and physical therapists, the Rolfer would assess particular kinds of injuries and suggest how treatment could be applied when appropriate. In fact, with our unique view of body mechanics, it is possible in some cases to predict where a budding athlete's structure will break down over time. The Rolfer's input in developing comprehensive training and rehabilitation programs is very valuable. Experience with sport injuries has suggested that many could be avoided or minimized, and recovery periods shortened

10. The results from the Hunt study indicate that a decrease in anxiety occurred after completion of the ten sessions of Rolfing. Further study is necessary to determine if there are specific neuromuscular patterns that correspond to anxiety or repressed emotions.
11. See the appendices for more information related to exercise and performance from a structural point of view.

by applying these principles. Rolfing ideas have wide-ranging implications and applications to sports which need to be considered by other specialists.

12

NOURISHING THE ROLFED BODY

Some people have problems with deposition of calcium in the knee. I've palpated spurs of calcium in the knee literally three-fourths of an inch long, so long that they inhibit movement. It's very painful. Yet, if we organize the lower leg and the upper leg, lo and behold, the calcium disappears. I've seen it disappear in a week. When there is flow through the tissue, it picks up whatever has been interfering, whatever had been deposited there through the slowing down of circulation.

I.P.R.

I define "health" as more than just the absence of disease. Health includes a concern for the quality of our lives now and efforts to prolong well-being throughout our life (prevention). This means living up to our potential and not accepting current definitions of "normal" as our standard. In my view, medical authorities certify us as "normal" if we are free from disease and symptoms. No concern is shown if our bodies are rigid and unbalanced and we live a sedentary, unfeeling life. The quality and quantity of our daily energy is a more accurate indicator of our level of wellness. Having a structurally balanced and responsive body is a major component of health. Eating the right foods, exercise, fresh air, water, sunlight, sleep, relaxation, positive thinking, meaningful work and personal relationships all contribute to total health. This chapter focuses on

the need for adequate nutrition as a major component of
health. The following information presents a plan for healthy eating and takes a brief look at the politics of agriculture, food marketing, and distribution.

In 1977, the Senate Select Committee on Nutrition
and Human Needs (headed by George McGovern) published its now infamous "Dietary Goals for the U.S."[1] This
study linked six of the ten leading causes of death, including cancer and heart disease, to the modern diet. The report stated that despite billions of dollars spent on research, modern medicine had failed to find a cure for such
illnesses as cancer, cardiovascular disease, diabetes, obesity,
multiple sclerosis and a host of other problems. It indicated the possibility that many of these conditons would be
preventable by maintaining a good diet. This stirred up the
food industry and started a whole cycle of activity aimed
at trying to discredit the implications of the report. The
food industry charged that the government was meddling
where it didn't belong and that such action was bad for
business. The administration countered that the people had
a right to unbiased information about food and that they
weren't getting it. McGovern and Dr. Mark Hegsted of the
Harvard School of Public Health (the author of the report)
were excited by the implications that simple changes in
diet will improve the health of Americans.[2] The report
recommended that Americans increase their consumption
of whole grains, vegetables, fruit and fish, while reducing
red meat, dairy products, refined sugar and salt. This battle
went on at various levels until Ronald Reagan was elected
president. With the de-regulation of industry as one of
Reagan's priorities, it is certain that many of the reforms

---

1. Since that time other Presidential and Congressional Committees have
been appointed to study the same problems and have reached the same conclusions. As yet no major funding has been allocated to implement any significant programs of nutritional change.
2. East West Journal, February 1981, pp. 40-47.

initiated as a result of the report will be lost. With the appointment of John Block (a Midwestern hog farmer) to Secretary of Agriculture, we have heard even less from the government on the "Dietary Goals" report. There is no reason to believe that any change in this position will be forthcoming with subsequent Secretaries of Agriculture.[3] Of course the politics of nutrition are global, as 800 million people in the world are starving, not for lack of agricultural capacity, but because of the politics of foreign aid and food distribution. The American Association for the Advancement of Science (AAAS) devoted a whole section of its last annual meeting to "National Impacts of Recommended Dietary Changes." The forum concluded that changes in our eating habits can have significantly beneficial effects on everything from land, fuel, water, and mineral use, to the cost of living, employment rates and the balance of international trade. Unfortunately, no programs have yet come forth from this meeting. A shift from animal products to vegetables and grains, for example, would reduce overall food costs and free up money for other sectors of the economy. Meats, for instance, cost five or six times as much as equivalent vegetable proteins. Consumption of animal foods adds approximately $4,000 to the average household budget, not counting the cost of increased medical care which may be needed when these foods are overconsumed. Production of animal food uses about 90% of all available agricultural land, and is largely responsible for excessive consumption of water and land resources in general. A 50% reduction of meat consumption could save half the energy, mineral resources and land, and one third of the water used in animal production. The story goes on and on and it is beyond the scope of this

3.   In addition, no input has come from the office of the Surgeon General. Instead, anti-smoking campaigns continue to get millions and nutrition is left to fend for itself.

chapter to go into the economics and politics of food production in greater detail. Suffice to say that a choice to
eat more simply has political and economic, as well as personal, implications.

We have rocketed into a technological age in the last
200 years. Along with this advancement has come increased
dependence on food which is grown far from where we live.
Before this time, we ate mostly what came from our region. The average person was accustomed to a relatively
limited assortment of foods. There were one or two
"staple" grains which, prepared in various ways, constitu-
ted total carbohydrate intake. This, coupled with locally
grown fruits and vegetables and some animal products
from domestic and wild sources, made up the bulk of the
diet. This diet could be considered "regionally simple."
It is reasonable to assume that the human body is designed
to run on a diet which is limited in variety and grown in
the area where a person lives. The tradition of a regionally
simple diet is in sharp contrast to the current state of in-
dustrialization of food processing from corporate farm to
individual tables. Greater quantites of imported and exotic
foods are now available in even the smallest towns in this
country.

When considering good nutrition we must take into
account the vital functions in a body. The body can be
viewed as a combustion system which depends on consumption of oxygen, proteins, and carbohydrates to produce heat and waste. In a combustion system, the ratio of
food to air consumption must be balanced with energy
expenditure. If the amount of food exceeds the air intake
or energy output, the body will begin to "load up" on its
waste products and lose efficiency. This could be likened
to a carburetor in a gasoline engine. Fuel and air are drawn
into the engine and burned, creating heat which is conver-
ted to mechanical energy to power the vehicle. The burned
fuel exhausts through the tail pipe. If the carburetor is

mis-adjusted so that too much fuel is added, the engine will sputter and spew unburned fuel out the exhaust. Conversely, if there is not enough fuel, the engine will starve and actually burn up over time. In a human these extremes are represented by a glutton at one end, and an anorexic at the other. Neither person uses their fuel efficiently. Every person must find the right balance between the quantity of food consumed and their ability to burn it. We must also look at the quality of fuel being "burned" to completely understand healthy eating. To discuss food quality, let's use the example of complex versus simple (refined) carbohydrates. We can use wheat, a staple grain, to illustrate this process. At one pole, we have "Essene" bread, discussed in the Bible. This is the most simple way to make a grain into an edible form. The wheat is covered with water and sprouted, then ground and made into dough with water. This mixture is left in the sun where the natural sugars ferment and the dough rises, creating a primitive bread. At the opposite pole we have bread that is the end product of a long process of refinement. The same whole wheat is ground into flour. It is then bleached to remove color and further processed into white flour. In order to make bread, it is necessary to add yeast, salt and water to make it rise. Then vitamins and minerals are added "12 ways" to bring the bread up to arbitrary "nutritional standards." This is baked to produce the familiar "white bread," which is basically pre-digested before it reaches the table. This means that some of the body's natural digestive processes are not used and assimilation of the bread is speeded up. The body uses the energy derived from this food very quickly. On the other hand, the primitive wheat bread begins its digestion in the mouth as the coarse wheat must be chewed thoroughly to release its food value. This process is continued in the stomach and intestines. The unrefined food burns more slowly and the energy lasts longer. Eating an apple versus drinking apple juice provides another example of the difference between whole and refined foods. The apple burns slowly and the energy produced lasts longer. The apple juice, an altered and "predigested" form is assimilated rapidly and the energy "peak" it produces passes quickly. Basically, I am comparing the assimilation rate of foods high in empty calories with foods that usually have less calories, but have more concentrated nutrients in their natural form. A person who consumes mostly processed and refined foods will have an energy pattern characterized by extreme highs and lows. The food is used quickly, creating a hunger for more of the same.

When Charlie came to be Rolfed one of his main complaints was that he never had enough energy.

"By the time I get home from work I don't have enough energy to exercise and release some of the tension I build up each day. So after dinner I end up watching television and before you know it I've fallen asleep in my chair."

Charlie starts each morning like many Americans, with two cups of coffee, a sweet roll and a glass of juice. "I'm trying to watch my weight, so I don't eat much at breakfast." By 10:00 a.m. Charlie is starting to feel a little groggy, so he usually has a Coke and a doughnut or another cup of coffee. Then he eats lunch around two and a half hours later. This usually involves more coffee or a soft drink, a hamburger or fried chicken and his favorite dessert — ice cream. Around 3:00 Charlie starts to feel a little low again, so he goes over to the vending machine and buys a candy bar so he can make it to quitting time. Charlie's dinners are a little better than his lunches, but they still include lots of refined foods with additives and preservatives, and sweets. Charlie's system is on a continual roller coaster ride. He goes from high stimulation to depression and is always in need of new energy. His body never has an opportunity to regulate itself. By the end of the day his system has given up. Only intensely stimulating food can give him "energy" at this point. Conversely, a person who eats unrefined, complex foods will have stable energy, less fluctuation in weight and less need for constant stimulation. Over time, this also means that he or she will have a more healthy digestive system. Eating the right kind of food can have a positive impact on your body's biochemistry, which significantly effects your mental and emotional health. Because our nervous systems operate through the transmission of electrochemical impulses, it would follow that balanced biochemistry supports balanced behavior.

"When diet is unbalanced . . . our brain function is disrupted. The ensuing disorder is both mental and physical: actions divorced from thoughts; ideas out of harmony with instinctive patterns and biological rhythms; limited perspectives; and limited self-control. The end result is the same: a reduction of performance and pleasure, feelings of depression, anxiety and fear (neurosis) and sometimes a sense of being disoriented or lost (psychosis)."[4]

"You are what you eat" is really a true statement.

Georgia is thirty-four years old and teaches elementary school. She came to me for some Rolfing and always complained of feeling groggy and having a hard time maintaining her concentration at work.

"After many years of frustration, nervousness and poor health I finally realized that refined foods, especially

---

4.   Saul Miller with JoAnne Miller, *Food For Thought*, 1979, Prentice-Hall, Englewood Cliffs, N.J., p. 3.

sugar and white flour, were causing my mental ups and downs. It's a real vicious cycle — you eat some sweets and feel high for a while, then you come tumbling down and get depressed. I start feeling paranoid, lose self-control and begin craving sweets. So I follow my cravings and eat some pastry or something and then feel high again. I'm now very conscious of what I eat and try to stick with whole foods whenever possible. This allows me to have a smoother energy pattern and I can avoid the peaks and valleys."

Thus far I have focused upon the politics of food, the importance of a regional diet, the need for a balance between food consumed and energy expended and the importance of eating foods in their natural state. We will now discuss more specifically how to eat in a balanced way. It must always be remembered that "magic diets" don't work for long. The program below focuses upon common sense and the maintenance of balance in eating habits.

A PLAN FOR HEALTHY EATING

1. Avoid foods containing artificial flavor and color, additives, preservatives and stabilizers. Eliminate most foods that are enriched, fortified, processed, canned, frozen or altered in any way. Become a label reader. You won't see much unadulterated food in the average supermarket. Find out what the ingredients are. Ask yourself "Is this food alive?" Remember that most of these products are treated to extend their shelf life and their commercial value, not their nutritional value.

2. Eat a higher percentage of raw foods. Over cooking destroys many of the essential enzymes necessary for proper digestion as well as water soluble vitamins and

nutrients. Purchase an inexpensive steamer and when possible steam rather than boil your foods. Save the broth for soups. It is a valuable source of nutrients.

3. I feel that a diet lower in animal products and higher in natural, unrefined carbohydrates will maintain optimum health.[5] Of course the body needs adequate protein. I suggest reducing the amount of animal protein normally recommended by the dietary "authorities" and substituting vegetable protein sources where possible. Over consumption of red meat is hard on the kidneys, pancreas, liver, adrenals, and gastro-intestinal tract (not to mention the pocketbook). Beans, tofu (soybean curd) and cheese are high in protein. Fruits, vegetables, nuts, seeds, and grains (cooked and sprouted) fill in the nutritional picture. Organically raised poultry and fish are also recommended.

4. Many people over eat. Consumption of food in excess of actual need will interfere with digestion, assimilation and proper elimination. Putrified foodstuffs in an over-full bowel can create gas, constipation or diarrhea, bloating and abdominal cramping. Eat until you feel 2/3 full, not until you feel stuffed.

5. Eat in a relaxed atmosphere. Chew your food slowly and thoroughly. If you are in a hurry or anxious or emotionally upset, it is best not to eat at that time.[6] Just take some liquids until you have settled down, then try some food. It will take patience to break old

---

5.   Nathan Pritikin, *The Pritikin Program for Diet and Exercise*, Bantam Books, 1979.
6.   Some recommend drinking a glass of lukewarm water with ½ to 1 tsp. of dry active yeast (not brewers or Torula) if you do not have time to eat properly. It will calm and alkalinize your stomach. See Henry Bieler, *Food Is Your Best Medicine*, Vintage Books, 1965.

habits, but the reward is soon felt in increased vitality and better digestion and elimination.

6. Different foods are processed by different parts of the body at different rates. Some attention should be paid to how you combine certain foods. Sugar and caffeine interfere with the digestion and assimilation of most foods. If you must eat these foods, take them alone at least two hours before or after meals. Consult the sources in the bibliography for more information on food combining, especially Gary Null's book *Food Combining Handbook,* and the Diamonds' *Fit for Life.*

7. Fasting once or twice a year will give your digestive system a well-deserved rest. If you have no experience with fasting, consult a knowledgeable physician or nutritionist as to procedure. I have used the process outlined by Paavo Airola[7] with great results.

8. Industrial farming, with its petroleum based pesticides and fertilizers, continues to deplete the soil. It is naive to think that even simple foods will have full nutritional value. Consider supplementing your diet with vitamins. They can serve as enrichment, but not replacement of good food.[8] Consult a certified nutritionist or doctor who is oriented toward these ideas. Most traditionally trained doctors know very little about nutrition and may suggest "one-a-day" supplements. Find someone else if you get this kind of advice!

9. I recommend that any change in diet be made gradual-

7.   Airola, *Are You Confused?* Health Plus Publishers, Box 22001, Phoenix, AZ, 85028.
8.   Be careful with over-consumption of vitamins. You may force your body to stop producing its own vitamins, minerals, and enzymes. (See Millers *Food For Thought.*)

ly. Too sudden a change may cause undue stress. Attitudes about food are formed early and run deep. Significant changes in eating habits may cause strong emotional reactions. Add a few new and simple foods at a time to your menu. Deal with your "addictions" and cravings one at a time. Don't try to clean house all at once.

It may take a couple of years for you to appreciate this greatly simplified way of eating. Get support and cooperation from others in your household. It's much easier when you have agreement about food purchasing and cooking. Don't become a "health food martyr." And don't be upset if you go on a "junk food" binge now and then. The anxiety is worse for you than the bad food.

This nutritional plan encourages balance, moderation, proper combining, self-regulation and an awareness of what you eat and how it may affect your behavior. This requires that you take complete responsibility for your nutritional well-being. There is not a lot of reinforcement for these ideas in a culture dominated by industry and media, yet good food and nutritional information are available. You have to look for it and care about it enough to find it. The model of nutrition I am suggesting is not faddist. It has been around for a long time. The closer to a primitive diet you can get, the more easily your body will function and the better you will feel.

One last point is worth mentioning. We are continuously bombarded with programs for keeping our weight under control. Few programs consider how much of the weight you lose comes from fat and how much comes from water and muscle loss. It's not how much you weigh that counts, but how much lean muscle you have in proportion to the amount of fat in your body.[9] If you just

9.   For a comprehensive discussion of being overweight vs. being overfat, see Covert Baily, *Fit or Fat*, Houghton Mifflin, Boston, 1978.

follow dietary programs concerned with losing pounds, the end result may be that you weigh less, but have the same amount of fat. You are not necessarily any more healthy, nor do you have any assurances that the weight will stay off.

Karen has been fighting a weight problem since she was thirteen. She has tried a series of weight reducing programs over the years, but none have been successful in keeping weight off for extended periods of time. "I can lose weight real easy, but six months later it's right back again and I have to start all over." At twenty-nine she has just about given up and is considering accepting being overweight. "Maybe I'll be happier if I just stay a little on the fat side and stop worrying about it!" After Rolfing, Karen's internal chemistry began to change and she found that she could keep weight off. A program of aerobic exercise and a change to a more natural diet enabled her to reduce her body fat. Her metabolism works much more efficiently and her weight is evenly balanced throughout her structure. The more fat you have, the less efficient you are at burning calories. The skin-fold calipers test is the simplest and cheapest way to measure your body fat. The most accurate method is underwater weighing, but it is expensive and difficult to do. A weight loss diet may burn more muscle tissue than fat. Effective weight loss, i.e. the burning of excess fat and the subsequent build up of muscle tissue, can only be maintained by a lifelong program of sensible eating coupled with aerobic exercise. Aerobic exercise establishes a more efficient pattern of body chemistry which tones your muscles and assists them in burning calories, even at rest. Stay away from the enticement of fad diets. In the short run you may lose weight and feel better, but in the long run you are actually training your body to be less efficient in burning calories.

13

ASCENDING TO HIGHER ORDER

When I talk about the upright placement of the head on the neck, I am also talking about using the evolutionary possibilities of human structure. Only by getting verticality in the body do you explore these possibilities. The minute you lose verticality, that minute you have lost the something plus that is available to humans.

I.P.R.

This book has focused upon the importance of achieving balance in all levels of being in order for us to truly be healthy. The need to develop an inner balance becomes increasingly important as the world continues to expand outward with scientific and technological advances. From this book's perspective, emphasis on outward progress must be continually balanced by inward development — the discovery and refinement of our selves. Unfortunately, most of us are not willing to balance between an internal and external reality. We want either to remain safe within our fantasies or "out" in the "real" world, focusing on superficial and external achievements.

Ida Rolf said "There is no sin but that which brings down the level of order and balance in the body." As we become more balanced, we are better able to see whether or not our actions add to or detract from our order and the order of other systems (people) around us. Development of self-regulation creates an inner-directed morality.

Internal equilibrium helps us to contribute to the health
of others, the social health of communities, healthy relationships with other countries and continents and, finally, to the health of the planet as a whole. The body is
our bridge between thought and action, the vehicle for
manifesting our intentions. The level of order in the body
influences our integrity and shapes the choices we make.
Many times Ida Rolf was heard to say "If you want to arrive at new conclusions, you must change your premises."
In the language of the new physics, she was talking about a
"paradigm shift" — a fundamental change in perspective
or world view which has a unitive effect upon people and
societal structure. Rolfing is much more than a mechanis-
tic discipline designed to order the body into a more efficiently functioning system. The hands-on application of
Rolfing and the principles which support it are themselves
a paradigm shift. Rolfing is a new collective map, a fundamental redefinition of how the body is organized in physical space, and how the various types of bodily organization influence how and what we feel and the way we be-
have. The aware client should be able to sense the manifestation of this shift in point of view through the Rolfer's
touch and eventually should experience this state in his
own body. Rolfing has the ultimate goal and opportunity
of allowing us to inhabit our bodies with a true sense of
dignity, that is, with mindfulness and compassion — the
conscious heart openly acting upon its feelings. In *Zen
Mind, Beginner's Mind*, Shunryu Suzuki calls this form of
embodiment, enlightenment, simply, an "ability to accept
things as they are."[1] A body at peace with itself is more
able to have the energy and clarity necessary for this degree of acceptance. A body in this state maintains a free
flow of breath which allows for relaxation in the system,

---

1.   *Zen Mind, Beginner's Mind*, Shunryu Suzuki, Weatherhill, N.Y. 1970.

leading to a reduction of "chatter," a clarity of mind which then calls us to greater sensitivity toward our fellow human beings. By examining human structure from a Rolfing perspective we may obtain a new understanding of life. This information has the power to transform the way we are in the world. We know now that we consist of something more than a collection of muscles and organs hanging on a brittle skeleton. We have found at the core of human structure a healthy, vibrating energy which can continuously re-order itself. This unique design allows us to fulfill our innate aspirations to become more, to stretch our potential, to seek beyond what is safe.

What of this tendency of the universe and all its creatures to seek ever increasing levels of order and complexity? The ideas of dissipative structures developed by physicist Ilya Prigogine have relevance here.[2] He suggests that most living systems are constantly re-making themselves and creating new energy. In his view, a healthy system is always in flux, re-ordering its elements into new patterns and interrelationships. Each system creates a newly functioning whole, more complex and more integrated than its predecessor. The Rolfing process reorders the elements of the human body into a newly effective pattern. The result is a human being who can function at higher levels. By ungluing blocked energy and allowing order to occur in a body, improvement in physical and emotional behavior will result. A highly ordered system, "unstable" in Prigogine's best sense of the word, is continuously in flux, allowing metabolism to freely regulate itself, toxins to be easily discharged and emotions and ideas to be processed quickly. Such a system encourages the creation of new thought forms and innovative uses of energy — a self-organized and self-regulated human being.

2.   See Marilyn Ferguson's *Aquarian Conspiracy* for a list of references which detail Ilya Prigogine's theories.

Rolfers often speak of ideal relationships for the various parts of the body. The critics suggest that the use of the term "ideal" is wrong because it implies something static and unchanging. I suggest that it's the critics who are stuck in their own outmoded perceptions of how the theories of Rolfing are actually practiced. Of course I cannot speak for the way all Rolfers do their work, but we do know that in many applications of Rolfing technology we see that helping people to experience ideal relationships in their bodies serves to expand, not limit their opportunities for efficient, purposeful and nourishing movement! We see that the critics have failed to keep pace with the evolution of the Rolfing work so they are presenting views which would have been more universally appropriate and accurate of the practice of Rolfing ten to fifteen years ago.[3,4] Judging from the incredible improvement that Rolf clients report in their levels of function and performance, the Rolfing ideals and applications through the hands-on work have hardly been experienced as static and limiting.

As a species we continue to exhibit a remarkable lack of insight. A recognition of the wholeness of life, the interrelationship of all things, still escapes us. We live in and through the flesh each waking and dreaming moment, yet we often treat our bodies as distant objects, disregarded until sickness or injury strike. In spite of our best intentions, we are beset with hate and fear, divided from ourselves, our fellow human beings, and the very earth we inhabit. We seem unable to comprehend our unque situation in which we find ourselves forever whirling around a relatively small sun on a rare and precious water planet. We are earthly entities bound in time, space and gravity in a physical universe. It is true that we have mastered flight

3.   Johnson, Don, "Somatic Platonism", SOMATICS Magazine, Vol. III, No. 1, Autumn 1980.
4.   Aston, Judith, "A Somatics Interview", SOMATICS Magazine, Vol. III, No. 1, Autumn 1980.

by mechanical means and some, at the height of ecstasy or in altered states, have flown without craft. And we have our dreams to ride, dreams which give us hope — hope of transcending our boundaries and becoming more than we conceptualize ourselves to be. But what of the aspiration in us to be more? "There is something in a person that reaches up," Ida Rolf said. "Up" is an elusive feeling which I contend is only experienced in a well ordered body. It can be described as a feeling of lightness and centeredness. The body may feel suspended, as if hanging by marionette strings. Rolfers are continually observing how an organized body expresses the feeling of "up" while simultaneously having to deal with the downward pull of gravity. As the flesh reaches higher levels of order and balance the person is more free to pursue their special quality of "up." The emotional quality of "up" allows us to take chances, to succeed, to fail, and to begin again. To re-order ourselves into a new energy unit, to become whole again, to resume function at a higher level of order and balance, to experience life as a process — where we are free once again to use the power of balance to ascend toward light.

In a Rolfed body, the forces of gravity become an asset instead of a disruptive influence. By relaxing self-imposed rigidities on body and mind, our fluid and plastic nature can be regained. Our resources of intuition, imagination, and self-healing become accessible once again. The choice is ours to make. We can experience our being with richness and vibrancy, or follow the dull and compulsive crowds. There will be some resistance to the positive transformation of the human body. It is also part of our nature to resist change and to stay with the familiar, regardless of how enticing the possibilities of change may appear. A stronger inner pulse prevails. It permeates all living forms. It is the intention of the universe and all its inhabitants to evolve — to follow the path toward light and the magnetism of self-transformation. By re-ordering the body into a balanced and more efficient energy system, Rolfing can make a unique contribution to the journeys of human transformation.

APPENDIX A
Glossary of Selected Terms

Anxiety: A "ready" state generated by thinking about past (or future-possible) disasters, betrayals, deadlines, etc. This mental activity stimulates changes in the body and its chemistry and prepares it for action.

Bio-mechanics: The scientific study of movement forces which arise from within or outside the body.

Cerebro-spinal fluid: A water envelope that bathes and nourishes the brain and spinal cord and cushions them from shock.

Compression: A state of shortness and thickening in tissue or joints when available length is not being used.

Core/Sleeve: The core is the non-flexed gravitational center of the body. The sleeve is the mass of the body operating around the core.

Extension: 1) Widens the angle formed by a joint. 2) Extending a muscle lengthens it.

Extrinsic: Structures that are on or close to the surface of the body. Example: the bicep is an extrinsic muscle. Also called the movement muscles.

Flexion: 1) To close the angle of a joint by bringing the parts closer together. 2) Flexing a muscle shortens it.

Horizontal: A plane of function in the body that inter-
sects the "line" forming a 90-degree angle with it. A knee
that functions as a hinge will operate in a horizontal plane.

Intrinsic: Those structures that lie deep within the body.
Example: the psoas muscle is an intrinsic muscle. Also
called the stabilizer muscles.

Line: The path of gravity's influence on the body-as-a-
whole. When a person is standing still, the "line" is perpen-
dicular to the surface they are standing on.

Matrix: 1) The internal cellular material of a tissue.
2) The environment in which an event takes place.

Posture: The position of the body structure(s) in space.
The form of the body as an expression of character. The
observable end result of Rolfing is improved posture.

Rotation: A process of turning on an axis. Two parts of
the body may be turned opposite one another around the
central line. These parts would be in rotation.

Span: The stretching of tissue across an underlying body
framework. If a body uses its available length in movement
the soft tissues span more effectively.

Stress: What differentiates stress from anxiety is that
stress includes physical insults and injuries as well as ima-
gined or potential trouble. One can stress oneself thinking
about trouble, misery, strain. Anxiety is a type of stress.

Structural Immaturity: Places in parts of the body that
appear younger than the rest. Usually the result of traumas
that "fix" the area in time. Usually associated with compression in that region. This state can also occur through-

out a body.

Structure: The various components that make up the physical body, i.e. bones, connective tissues, muscles, organs.

Tone: A quality of tissue that reflects the chemical and energetic process going on in it. 1) Hypotone would be looser than normal for the body type or region. 2) Hypertone would be tighter or more dense than normal for the area or body in question.

Torsion: A twist between two adjacent parts of the body, usually across a joint along a complementary axis.

APPENDIX B
Rolfing Movement Integration

Movement Education for Everyday Life
by
Heather Wing[1]

A secretary who suffered from chronic severe headaches learned how to sit, phone, and type more efficiently, and her headaches disappeared.

A large man received feedback that he was overpowering. During the course of a Rolfing Movement class he learned a softer self-presentation, more true to his warmhearted nature, and also found relief from the chronic lower back pain that had resulted from his former stance.

A woman in her seventies used a cane and brace to help her walk with a dysfunctional right leg. She was tense from the effort of walking, tired easily, and had pain in the left side of her back. In her Movement sessions she learned new ways of balancing and swinging her right leg that eased the pain in her left side and relieved much of the stress of walking.

A tall young man, coming out of an upbringing that "humbled" him and taught him to carry his head down, couldn't get a job. It took a number of Movement sessions before he was comfortable carrying his head on top of his body, eyes level. The change in the angle of his head

---

1. Heather Wing is a Certified Rolfing Movement Teacher and Movement Instructor at the Rolf Institute of Structural Integration in Boulder, Colorado.

greatly altered his appearance as well as his self-confidence; and in the next week he got an excellent job, far better than he had previously hoped or reached for.

A two-month-old baby turned his head only to the left and reached out only with his left hand. A Movement Teacher played with him and gave his mother some guidelines for carrying and relating to him, and he soon regained balanced movement in head and arms.

With the help of a Movement Teacher, a computer technician who got backaches while working analyzed how he related physically to his computer. He found, in the process, that he did not want to relate to it at all, and changed jobs.

A therapist learned new ways of sitting that helped him be more available to his clients. A woman in her forties had a tense, strained face that made her look older than her years. Her Movement Teacher helped her become aware of her tensions, and showed her ways to ease them, particularly around her eyes and jaw. Not only her face, but her whole body softened, and she now moves more easily, has more energy, and looks younger.

The director of a private elementary school realized in the course of her Movement sessions that the way the children in her school were sitting as they learned to write was hampering their learning. She invited her Movement Teacher to the school and together they evaluated her furniture, reviewed some basic principles of sitting, and created a supportive environment for the children's writing classes.

A massage therapist felt her identity blurring with that of her clients. Following a day's work she often felt confused and fatigued. During her Movement sessions she came to have a clearer sense of her own center and how to work from it without giving it away. Her sense of herself was greatly enhanced, and her relationship with her clients clarified, and she found that she had far more energy for her work.

A handyman discovered efficient ways of lifting heavy objects that took the strain off his lower back.

These are some experiences of people who have studied Rolfing Movement Integration.

Rolfing Movement Integration is a system of movement education for everyday life based on principles developed by Dr. Ida P. Rolf, the creator of Rolfing. Its applications are as various as human activities and problems. Its goal is to assist people to move easily and gracefully through their daily lives.

Dr. Rolf based her work on several insights important to our understanding of movement. The first is that we all live and grow in the gravitational field. Gravity is one of the strongest and most reliable forces in incarnate existence. We have the option of learning to move harmoniously with gravity, thus allowing it to become a unifying and energizing force for us. Or we may live in resistance to it, and find in the end that gravity is stronger, and tears us down and apart.

Secondly, Dr. Rolf realized that we are segmented creatures, each a whole made up of many parts, balancing vertically in the gravitational field. She emphasized the importance of connective tissue, or fascia, in this segmented vertical body. Our connective tissue forms a three-dimensional net or web that goes all around the body under the skin; all through the body wrapping and connecting every bone, organ, vessel, nerve and muscle. Just as the whole spider web moves and changes when an insect lands in one corner, so our whole fascial net responds to influence upon any part of it. As we balance more or less imperfectly, it is the connective tissue which holds us together and takes the stress of our imbalance. The condition of the fascia, whether and where it is free or tight, scarred or responsive, shapes us and determines the relationship of our parts to each other and to the gravitational field. Further, the whole pattern of relationships becomes a physical statement of our emotional realities and the way we express ourselves in our lives.

Dr. Rolf also learned that these patterns can change, that traumatized connective tissue can be softened and released, that stressful movement patterns can be eased, and that the whole person can live more comfortably and healthfully as he comes into greater harmony with gravity.

The work that developed from her vision has two modalities. Rolfing is the manipulation of the connective tissue focused on evoking a balanced structure[2], and Rolfing Movement Integration re-educates movement habits with the focus of evoking balanced function.

In both disciplines we play continually between two foci. We look at the individual before us. What are this person's limitations, activities, and goals? A woman who has sight in only one eye may need to balance her head differently than a person with sight in two eyes. A student of meditation may need assistance in sitting comfortably crosslegged for long hours and also some guidance in how to balance his pelvis when he gets up to move about in the world again. A man doing heavy work needs information about how to lift efficiently.

People come to us from many walks of life, wearing bodies of many shapes and moving in various ways. Sometimes body shapes and movement patterns obscure the people within and frustrate them in the pursuit of their goals. We seek to help each one find a body and a way of moving that will serve well in the life that he or she chooses, and express who she or he really is.

Unique as we are, we are, at least physically, more-alike than we are different. We each have two arms, two legs, and a segmented spine with a head on top. We all move about vertically in the gravitational field. Dr. Rolf

2. Articles and books on Rolfing can be obtained through the Rolf Institute, P.O. Box 1868, Boulder, Colorado 80306.

found that certain arrangements of body parts give maximum support, and that organizing the structure around a central axis allows the body a lift that reverses gravity's usual downward pull. Over the years, she developed these practical discoveries into a system of principles that form the basis of Rolfing and Rolfing Movement Integration.

So we consider both the individual's unique pattern, needs, and goals and those basic principles that affect all human structure.

MOVEMENT PATTERNS

One of the ways we most clearly express our uniqueness is in our movement patterns. Each of us has our own way of breathing, bending, reaching, walking. How we move is a vital expression of our histories, our personalities, our very selves.

We develop our movement patterns from conception, the moment we enter the gravitational field. As we grow in the womb, we adapt to our mother's structure and activities. Birth shapes us strongly; and from then on physical and emotional influences, and our response to them, continue to shape our bodies, our movements and our ways of being in the world.

A baby may learn to turn his head to only one side because his crib is placed in a certain relationship to light and interesting objects in the room and he is always laid with head at the same end. A little girl begins ballet at an early age, and for years models herself after her teachers and learns the ballet patterns. Even if she later decides to become a policewoman, she may for the rest of her life turn her feet out and arch her back like a ballet dancer. A child who is continually bullied, either emotionally or physically, may develop an attitude of cringing which stays with him into adulthood. Another child may develop asthma in response to the stresses of her life, and even after stresses and asthma have passed, retain a pattern of shallow, panicky breathing that affects her posture, her activities and her general health. A boy may fall on his roller skates and twist his coccyx. As he grows older his walk may change as a result, his legs and upper body compensate, creating a system of tensions and counter-tensions that may cause him pain and limit his movement for the rest of his life. We each have our own unique story, our own combination of events and responses. Movement patterns affect our degree of physical comfort, our ways of relating to other people and objects in our environment, even our feelings about ourselves. They express us intimately and powerfully. As we come to understand them and find new options for patterns which frustrate or defeat us, we are transforming not only the way we might carry our head or pick up a wastebasket, but our whole way of being in the world.

Let us now look at some of the basic principles underlying Rolfing Movement, for it is to them that we turn as we seek new options for stressful movement patterns.

SEVEN BASIC PRINCIPLES

These principles are very much interwoven, not so much separate ideas as different aspects of one idea — seven facets of one jewel, or seven different colored threads woven into one tapestry.

Core

We use the word "core" to talk about the central axis that is so vital to Dr. Rolf's vision of a body organized harmoniously with gravity. It is also sometimes called the "Rolf line." We visualize it running through the center of the body from the crown of the head down just in front of the spine, through the insides of the legs and the arches of the feet.

Physically the core is composed of a network of deep muscles lying close to the central axis. As we learn to move more from these deep muscles, often unused in the uneducated body, we are able to release tension in external muscles whose line of pull is not as well oriented to do the jobs we ask of them. Our movement, and we ourselves, become literally, physically more centered.

The experience of the core can be explored through a number of images. It can be seen as a channel for the force of gravity which moves through us both downward and upward, grounding us through the soles of our feet and at the same time giving us lift and lightness.

We may visualize a fountain, a single jet of liquid light, rising from the center of the earth, upward through the core, bubbling out the top of the head, and falling down all around us. So we may touch in to the experience of the core lifting and the outer body resting down, relieved at last of the strain of holding us up.

We may feel the core as part of a great circle, the circle so great that our tiny portion of it seems almost, but not quite, straight — for nothing in nature is truly straight. This great circle also passes through the center of the earth connecting us strongly to the source of our gravitational field.

Sometimes the experience of the core is found first in the lying position as we imagine the breath moving like a gentle wave up and down the front of the spine and into the head.

Some of us come to know the core as the source of our inner strength and light and/or as the channel which connects us to sources of light and strength beyond.

Whatever the image, bringing awareness to the core gives us more physical ease and a new sense of strength and quiet power. We begin the transition from defending ourselves with external muscle tension to trusting for our strength in centeredness and balance.

Dynamic Balance

Dynamic balance point is that point in space where the vertical body feels lightest. It is the moment of maximum lift and maximum potential to move with equal ease in any direction and into any kind of action. We become like an upwardly-poised pendulum with the possibility of three-dimensional swing, containing its power in its very lightness.

Paradoxically, dynamic balance is both a point in space that can be found and felt with a certain ping! and not a point at all, but a process. As we find the support of gravity, tension releases. When tension releases, structure changes, and when structure changes so does the point of dynamic balance. For example, when a young woman with a deeply arched lower back finds her lightest place, she will be leaning slightly forward to balance the backward swing of her pelvis. A boy with his pelvis tucked down and under him will find his lightest place leaning slightly back. (The more nearly the pelvis is horizontal and the weight blocks aligned one over the other, the more vertical and the lighter the lightest place will be.) The young woman with the arched back, when she comes to her lightest place, may be able to let go of some of her lower back tension and then find her balance a little further back. The boy may feel a lift that allows his pelvis to come more under him and moves him slightly forward. We play with balancing, subtly adjusting our alignment, until ping! we are there! then more release, more adjustment and we are there again.

The experience of dynamic balance has many facets. In the feeling of being lifted and at the same time letting go, there is a sense of peace, of coming to rest; hence, we sometimes call it "home space." At times there comes a simultaneous release of both physical holding patterns and the emotional patterns attached to them. With this release may come an experience of clarity, detachment, of being available to respond in new ways on all levels; so sometimes we call it "clear space." It is not always clear space. Other times it is the moment in which held emotion is set free to flow and so it may be "sorrow space" or "anger space" or "joy space" until the flow has passed through.

The quality of dynamic balance can be carried into action. A martial artist speaks of the calm at the center of the cyclone which he feels in the midst of a four-man attack. A massage therapist has an experience of channeling energy. A mother of several pre-school children rests in a quiet centeredness that maintains her through the late-afternoon chaos. All connect, in their own way, to the vital poise, containing both ease and power, which is the essence of dynamic balance.

Support

Underlying dynamic balance is the principle of support. The more nearly our body parts are aligned one over the other, the lighter dynamic balance point becomes.

Our logo is a metaphor comparing the segments of the body (head, thorax, pelvis, legs) with a pile of blocks. When these blocks are piled securely over each other, the structure is stable, the weight of each part carried through the parts below to the earth. When one block is pushed forward, another back, a third one twisted, the structure becomes unstable in direct proportion to the amount of displacement of the blocks. We need to add to the image the fascial net going around and through all the blocks, and then we can see clearly how an unstable structure torques and strains our connective tissue, and how encouraging the blocks to rest one over the other can ease that stress.

The pile of blocks is a static image, but as we move

into action we find the essential principle is the same; the weight of each body part must be carried through to the earth, or we feel the lack of support for that part as tension in the connective tissue.

We use what we call the "rocker principle" to teach support for action. We create a rocker, like the rocker on a rocking chair, at the base of our support. The rocker may be from one foot to the other, from the hips if we are sitting, or from one knee to the other foot. Action is initiated with a rocking movement from the rocker. Without a rocking movement from the base of support, some part of the body must move away from the action to counterbalance it, thus breaking the flow of support through to the ground. With a rocker, the major weight blocks of head, thorax, and pelvis are allowed to remain in supportive alignment.

So a man leans over to pick up a heavy object with his feet side by side. His lower body does not participate in the action; he has no rocker. His pelvis goes back for counterbalance, leaving his shoulders hanging out in space and the muscles of his lower back holding not only his body weight but the weight of the object he is lifting. If he puts one foot forward as he lifts, that foot is under the shoulders and carries the weight downward, the legs lever to assist the action of lifting, and no single part is overworked.

When the body comes into balance, the whole person feels more secure. The feeling of being "left hanging" is both physically and psychologically diminished. Support becomes a reality on many levels.

Responsiveness

When the body is well supported, then the fascial net is free to respond. Movement flows through it like ripples on water, circling outward from the place of impulse. So the movement of the breath, beginning in the diaphragm and the muscles between the ribs, can be felt throughout the body. The shoulders float out and away from the expanding lungs, the head moves slightly, the pelvis widens and the sacrum drops. Dr. Rolf said "The arches breathe." It is not that there are lungs in the feet, but that the fascial net knows the breathing movement even as far away as the feet.

Life is movement. Once we've experienced the lightness of dynamic balance, we discover we are never completely still even when sitting quietly. There is always subtle intrinsic movement, the inner dance of breath flow, blood beat, digestive swirl, and the continuous delicate fine-tuning of our relationship with gravity.

We are only still when we hold ourselves still, and unfortunately most of us are all too adept at that. We still ourselves when emotion overwhelms us in moments when we feel it is not appropriate to express emotion. Who will release his jaw when tears threaten in a competitive situation? If we have been taught, as most of us have, that it is rarely appropriate to express emotion, our self-imposed stillness becomes a rigorous part of our daily pattern. Such emotional holding stresses the fascial net, eventually contributing to imbalance. The more imbalanced we feel physically, the more insecure we feel psychologically, the more we hold, and so it spirals.

We also still ourselves with effort. We furrow the brow with mental concentration, lock the jaw, tense the abdomen, or hold the breath with physical exertion. If our lifestyle is one of effort, such patterns may be so deeply set in us that we are no longer aware of other options.

Holding, however it originates, interrupts the flow of movement which then impacts in much the same way as a wave breaks against a cliff. A child may fold his head down and tight against the upward expansion of his inhalation (impact at the neck), a student may hold her whole body still except for her arm when writing (impact at the shoulder), or a runner may hold his upper body back and down against the upward flow of movement from his legs (impact in the lower back). Tension and awkwardness result.

Rolfing Movement focuses on bringing such holding patterns to consciousness and introducing new options. Our goal is to free the fascial net to respond without interruption to movements both internal and external, large and small — the almost imperceptible breath of the meditator or the swing of an axe. Such a responsive attitude in the flesh teaches us also how to be more responsive to the changing conditions of our lives.

Lengthening

We soar by grounding. Within the core we feel the creative tension between the downward pull and the upward lift of gravity. As we open into our length, we gain a feeling of spaciousness, of more fullness in all dimensions.

Activity in the uneducated body almost always results in shortening. We contract the same muscles again and again, never fully releasing them until we feel tight and fatigued. Sometimes we instinctively stretch them to regain the comfort of length, but then go back again to moving in the same shortening ways.

In Rolfing Movement, one of our goals is to learn to lengthen rather than shorten with each movement. We learn to ease tension in our joints so our limbs can swing freely. We learn to lengthen the core, opening the lower spine with each step of our walking, extending the core as we reach forward. We allow the spine to make long open arcs as we bend down to pick up an object or reach up to a high shelf. Even with the breath the core grows longer as the head floats up and the sacrum drops. The more we learn to carry out our daily life activities with length, the more energy we have, since lengthening continually refreshes us.

When we move with length, we allow a healthier environment for our insides. An open spine permits better circulation and innervation throughout the body. Internal organs function better when not impinged upon by surrounding structures. Dr. Rolf spoke of the "peace of length." In a very physical sense, the pressure is off, and the whole person feels the relief.

Integrity of Movement

The whole body participates in the direction of intention.

We often pull ourselves in opposite directions. A man reaches out to shake hands, and pulls his chest back. A young girl walks forward, swinging her right knee sideward and her left shoulder back. A housewife reaches up, pulling her chest down against her upward reach. Such contradiction of direction within the body creates/expresses a contradiction of intention which is confusing both to the person moving in opposite directions, and to any with whom he might relate. Contradiction of direction in movement also creates physical stress and sometimes pain.

As we learn to bring our whole body into focus on an action, whether routine or of special significance, our intention clarifies and all our energies are available to fulfill that intention. Quite literally, we no longer fight ourselves. Focusing the whole body on an action almost always involves bringing the whole self to it. We suddenly find ourselves present in a startlingly total way. A deep sense of peace, order and inner strength results. We come into harmony with ourselves.

Harmony With Gravity

We use gravity in all our actions, moving through dynamic balance point into that relationship with gravity which will most assist us with our task. Weight, leverage, and momentum become daily life tools. We no longer have to accomplish everything out of our limited personal strength.

So a Rolfer rocks his body forward over his hands; his
falling weight supplies the force he needs, his shoulders
stay open and relaxed, and his touch is gentle and pene-
trating. A gardener rocks her body weight over her shovel
to dig in and swings from one foot to the other as she
throws manure into her newly turned plot. A dancer dis-
covers that his leg is lighter and swings higher when his
thorax is well balanced over his pelvis. All receive help
from gravity in various ways.

We learn how gravity functions and how to avoid re-
sisting it. We lean forward to climb stairs or hills, so we
are not pushing our body weight directly up. (Gravity
comes directly down.) We roll to one side to get out of
bed, instead of sitting up against gravity's pressure on the
whole length of our body. When we bend over, we let our
heads fall, instead of unnecessarily holding that weight
against gravity's pull. It is resistance to gravity that causes
awkwardness. Harmony results in ease, flow, and grace.

Learning how to harmonize with gravity teaches us
gradually how to live more harmoniously in other aspects
of our lives. Tools for dealing with the world change from
clenched determination and combat to balanced centeredness and quiet intention. As we give up fighting everything
around us, we find we have more energy for work, play,
relationships, and creative pursuits.

LEARNING ROLFING MOVEMENT

Learning Rolfing Movement involves three basic processes. The first is awareness, discovering how we actually
move, breathe, work, play and handle stress. The second
step is that of letting go; of comfortingly familiar but uncomfortable ways of moving, stereotyped body images,
physical defenses, attitudes. The third step is exploring
new options. These steps rarely happen in linear sequence.

Sometimes their occurrence is almost simultaneous; often there is a spiral effect. New options lead to new awareness, to more releasing, to still more new options.

Private Sessions

One way to learn Rolfing Movement is in a series of private sessions. These sessions begin with client and teacher exploring the present movement patterns of the client. They talk, reviewing the client's history of injuries and illnesses, his feelings about his body, his ways of expressing stress, his activities, and his expectations for the series of sessions. Various techniques may be used to record the client's patterns at the beginning; Polaroid photographs, video, and/or drawings that the client makes of his own body (a surprisingly accurate index of body image). These are studied by the client and teacher together to increase their understanding of the client's patterns. The client walks and becomes aware of how each individual part of his body moves in relation to others, how his weight is carried, what parts are held still as he moves, what parts unsupported. This experience can be related back to the client's history and to the pictures studied earlier.

Once client and teacher have a clear understanding of the client's present movement patterns, activities, and feelings about his body, they begin to explore new movement possibilities for him. During the series of sessions, usually eight or ten in number, the client explores individual parts of his body and certain basic activities in depth. A series of sessions usually covers breathing, sitting, pelvis, head and face, legs and feet, shoulders and arms, and any special activities the client is involved in. The teacher is sensitive to the activities, needs and personality of the client and arranges these phases of the work to best suit that individual's unfolding.

In each session the client experiences the processes of awareness, letting go, and new options. The awareness is usually gained by simply walking or breathing or doing a familiar movement to see what happens with a particular body part. Letting go is guided with breath, imagery, firm gentle touches from the teacher, and simple movements that, when repeated, encourage the releasing of specific muscle groups. New options are gained through movements designed to re-educate a part of the body into more efficient use, and a continued awareness of supporting that part in relation to other parts and to the field of gravity. Throughout, freer and more balanced possibilities are explored for the basic human movements of walking, breathing, standing, and sitting. These movements are also used as ways of integrating individual parts into the whole.

Out of this experience the client learns a gently simple series of centering movements that can be used at home to ease stress, restore balance after injury, and continue movement re-education initiated in the sessions.

Classes

Although private sessions provide the most sheltered and focused situation for learning Rolfing Movement, classes are also available, kept small so students can receive individual attention. Students learn the same basic material they would in private sessions, as well as having the opportunity to see how Rolfing principles apply in the movement habits of their classmates. The class environment is warm and supportive, and students help each other as part of their own learning process.

Special Interest Workshops bring Rolfing principles into practical application to a wide range of activities. They are offered for runners, yoga students, musicians, carpenters, mothers with small babies, office workers, massage therapists, or any other group that might wish to join together to find ways to make their common activity easier and more enjoyable.

Rolf Rhythms is a series of lively yet relaxing exercises

developed by Rolfing Movement Teachers and designed to evoke awareness of Rolfing principles at the same time that they strengthen, improve muscle tone and coordination, deepen breathing and extend flexibility. Rolf Rhythms is usually taught in a class situation, and designed for individual practice.

Rolfing and Rolfing Movement

Rolfing Movement can be learned by itself or in conjunction with a series of Rolfing sessions. The two disciplines are at once independent and complementary.

Rolfing can enhance Rolfing Movement by freeing the structure so the client has more possibilities to work with. Rolfing Movement can enrich Rolfing by allowing time and focus to enlarge upon the educational process begun in Rolfing sessions. Through Movement, the client is assisted in actually manifesting the changes of Rolfing in day-to-day life.

A client deciding to enter into both processes may do them either in sequence or concurrently. If Movement comes first, the client enters into her Rolfing process an informed and enthusiastic co-worker, well acquainted with her patterns, her restrictions, and the possibilities of better balance. When her Rolfer comes to a difficult place in her structure, she is less likely to shrink back feeling "Oh, no!", more likely to respond "Thank goodness! I am finally going to get help with that!" If Rolfing comes first, the client comes to his Movement sessions with a far freer structure, more options available. Perhaps most ideal is alternating sessions of Rolfing Movement and Rolfing. This arrangement gives the Rolfer, client and Movement Teacher an opportunity to work closely together, and Movement sessions can prepare for or follow up on Rolfing sessions with effective immediacy.

SOME RESULTS OF
ROLFING MOVEMENT INTEGRATION

Most clients find that Rolfing Movement gives them new ways to handle and diminish stress. Often the first step is for the client to realize she is under stress. One young woman wrote at the end of her series of private sessions, "Looking back, I never realized the pain I was in until I acknowledged its presence and location and it started to leave." For many clients chronic, even acute, pain is eliminated as they learn how to support their actions physically. Others discover that Rolfing Movement helps most with emotional stress, as they find in their more stable relationship to gravity a new sense of inner strength and self-acceptance. The core breath is a practice many use, like a gentle physical meditation, to regain perspective and handle strong flows of emotion.

Rolfing Movement clients often start to feel better about how they look. Even without weight loss, a person looks slimmer when a tipped pelvis is balanced and the abdomen no longer spills out unsupported. Lines of stress and tautness in the face, tight jaws, straining eyes can all be eased as the client learns to balance the head and release the muscles of the face. Tense, awkward or heavy movement can be replaced by elegance and grace.

Coming to understand the connection between attitude and carriage is another powerful effect of Rolfing Movement. Clients learn that how they move affects how they feel, and that they have options. They can choose, by altering their body stance, to withdraw or reach out. They begin to understand how their bodies communicate and make choices about what they want to say. They discover that considering a problem in a slumped-down position can make it seem overwhelming, whereas considering the same problem in the vitality of dynamic balance can open new and hopeful possibilities.

Changes in self-presentation occur. One of our goals is to bring the outer presentation into harmony with the inner being. Often outmoded patterns of movement confuse and inhibit true expression of a person's present self. A competent professional woman may still hold her head low, look up out of the tops of her eyes and speak in a high voice like a little girl. Attitudes of childhood defiance (lower back arches, knees locked, head thrown back) which might have been an absolutely essential and vital statement of "I am!" from a small person in a big, overpowering world, may have quite the opposite effect when they linger on in a man of thirty-five, causing him physical pain and limiting his personal effectiveness. Exploring options for mature self-presentation frees the client to be and express who he presently is, and increases his credibility and self-confidence.

Changes in jobs and personal relationships may sometimes occur as a result of the Rolfing Movement process. As clients get more in touch with the sources of their stresses and come into a more powerful and accepting sense of themselves, they become less tolerant of painful or frustrating situations, more confident that they can change them.

EVOLUTION OF
ROLFING MOVEMENT INTEGRATION

Although Rolfing Movement is a recent development in its present name and form, movement education associated with Rolfing has a long history.

Dr. Rolf began to develop Rolfing in the early 1930's, working in the beginning as much with movement as with manipulation. Always, as Rolfing evolved, she insisted that it was an educational process. When she began to train Rolfers formally, she defined the goals of each Rolfing session primarily in terms of movement. She developed a series of balancing exercises to be done after Rolfing to continue and maintain the changes made, and taught these exercises to all her graduating Rolfing practitioners.

Dorothy Nolte, coming out of a background of nursing and human relations, trained as a Rolfer in the late 50's. She soon saw that her clients wanted to do something for themselves after their Rolfing sessions. Working closely with Dr. Rolf, she developed Dr. Rolf's movements into an independent educational system called Structural Awareness. She began teaching Structural Awareness in 1962 in both classes and private sessions; and during the past twenty years, has taken Structural Awareness into a wide variety of educational settings. Her work is carried on by Rachel Harris, who trained extensively with Dorothy and has recently developed research evaluating the effectiveness of Structural Awareness and a self-study program composed of cassette tapes and booklets.[3]

Judith Aston, a dancer, teacher, and movement facilitator for Gestalt Therapy, trained as a Rolfer in the late sixties. Working with Dr. Rolf, Dorothy Nolte, and then independently, she created a system of movement education called Rolf/Aston Structural Patterning. She began training teachers of Structural Patterning (called Patterners) in 1971. For several years Judith worked closely with the Rolf Institute developing patterning workshops for Rolfers and Rolfing students, as well as training Patterners. However, by the mid-seventies, her work began to take a direction which she felt was not compatible with Rolfing, and in 1977 she resigned from the Rolf Institute and renamed her work Aston-Patterning.[4]

3. For more information about Structural Awareness contact Dr. Rachel Harris, Suite 214, 1550 S. Dixie Hwy., Coral Gables, Florida, 33146.
4. For more information about Aston-Patterning, contact Aston-Patterning Consultants, Inc., P.O. Box 114, Tiburon, California 94920.

Rolfing Movement Integration began in 1978 when two former Patterners, Gael Switzer and I, collaborated with Rolfing Teachers Peter Melchior and Emmet Hutchins to create a movement curriculum for Rolfing students. In the fall of 1978 five other former Patterners gathered with Gael and me to share work and sort from all our varied approaches those concepts and techniques which would best evolve Rolfing in the movement modality.

By June 1979, we had formed the Movement Committee. Our group had grown, as other former Structural Patterners joined us. We had been teaching classes for Rolfing students for more than a year, had created a place for ourselves in the political structure of the Rolf Institute, designed a training program for new Movement Teachers. That fall we launched our first training program. Membership in the Rolf Institute was granted to nine Movement Teachers on January 1, 1980 and to nine others within the next year, six of whom were graduates of our first Training Program.

We presently offer, as well as the services to the public described earlier in this article, a number of professional programs within the Rolf Institute. These include movement classes for Rolfing students in their basic training, workshops for certified Rolfers, a full training program for the certification of new Movement Teachers, and Movement Exchange Workshops and an Annual Conference for certified Movement Teachers.

Rolfing Movement is an alive and growing art. It is nourished by all three of the forms that preceded it. Dr. Rolf's vision is the root and source of our work. Dorothy Nolte was the first to develop an independent system of Rolfing-based movement education that could be taught to people new to Rolfing as well as those who had been Rolfed. We are indebted to Judith Aston for her rich development of the concept of responsiveness, for her work in helping Rolfers use their bodies more effectively, and for her application of Rolfing principles to daily life activities.

Our work continues to develop as we gain more understanding of human movement in the gravitational field. As individual teachers, we continue to explore Rolfing concepts in our own bodies and activities. We dialogue and exchange work with each other, our Rolfer colleagues, and teachers in related body-work and movement disciplines. Most of all we listen to the teaching, in whatever form it comes, of each client who comes through our doors.

Jocelyn's Experience

Jocelyn is a graduate student at the University of Colorado and works as a housekeeper. She is a slender, quiet, competent woman in her early thirties with large sparkling brown eyes, a wide warm smile and a slightly off-beat sense of humor. She had had twenty sessions of Rolfing, had practiced meditation and Tai Chi for several years, and had made some radical changes in her diet before she came to work with me. All of these activities had dramatically improved her well-being, and she still had some difficulties she wanted help with.

In her first session, as we sat together to learn about her movement patterns, she reported being uncomfortable standing, having pain in her lower back and tension and discomfort in her shoulders, especially when vacuuming or studying. She was unable to study for long periods. Severe bronchial problems since childhood and recent sinus surgery had left her with considerable fear about being able to breathe. Her health, though much improved, was still unreliable. Under stress her breathing tightened, tension spiraled, she had nightmares and headaches, and often became sick.

As we walked together, we found that she leaned back

from the waist leaving her chest unsupported. Her lower back was short and tight and she tended to pull her shoulders up and forward around her chest. She usually carried her head and eyes down.

Once we had a sense of her patterns, we began by focusing on her breath. We worked together, I using gentle hand pressure on her chest, simple instructions and imagery to guide awareness, she allowing breath into new places in her upper chest and releasing some of the fear that had accumulated there when she gasped for air as a child. I adjusted her head which was, even in the lying position, bent toward her chest, creating a still cramped place in the front of her neck. At first she felt uncomfortable and somewhat exposed with her chin higher, but soon discovered that her breath opened up even more, given the extra space, and that her neck was able to respond with a slight internal movement. Finally I guided her breath to her core, using the image of a wave of liquid light flowing up and down the front of her spine. Throughout the process her breathing deepened and slowed and her color heightened.

After a brief review of the steps we had taken to come to an easier, fuller breath, I guided her to sitting. Her usual sitting pattern involved leaning back slightly, so we balanced back and forth between that position and dynamic balance point to see how her angle in gravity affected her breath. She found that in her leaning-back position her chest was unsupported and she had to tighten it to hold herself up. This left little freedom to breathe in the chest. In dynamic balance, however, her breath flowed easily into the new spaces she had opened while lying down.

Standing and walking she again explored dynamic balance point, contrasting it with her familiar pattern and discovering how the breath moved in each position. Her experience of her core while lying down and breathing assisted her in feeling supported in the newness of verticality.

We ended by finding ways she could support her shoulders while vacuuming. She walked out in her new-found balance, her color high.

In the following week she was very conscious of her leaning-back pattern and how it affected her breathing. On several occasions, when she was tense or fatigued, she lay down and practiced her core breath and found that the deeper slower breath calmed and refreshed her.

In her second session she reviewed and deepened her experience of her breath and discovered that the way she carried her head and eyes affected not only her breathing, but her sense of openness to connect to other people. Finding dynamic balance point now gave her support for her head to be up and her eyes straight ahead. She could still choose the option of lowering them when she did not wish to connect. We explored these contrasts, walking toward each other across the room and feeling what it was like to meet in each of these ways.

In her third session, which was focused on sitting, Jocelyn gained a much clearer understanding of dynamic balance point. She discovered how allowing her whole body to be balanced and responsive to the movement of writing alleviated stress in her shoulders and allowed her to breathe more fully while she studied.

As the weeks went by she found she could study for longer periods without fatigue. She would often find herself hunched up in her familiar way, chest dropped and shoulders taut; but once she noticed, she could adjust her chair, rediscover her balance, breathe deeply and begin again refreshed. Vacuuming no longer hurt her back.

Her fourth session focused on her head and pelvis. She learned to breathe very gently into her sinuses. This was difficult at first because of the trauma left by her sinus surgery; but as she gained more control of it, she found she could use it to open her sinuses when she became congested and avert a sinus headache. The pelvic work gave her more length in her spine and a gentle pelvic movement she could use to ease tightness in her lower back.

In the sessions that followed she gained greater under-standing of how the joints of her toes, ankles, knees, and hips could work together for an easier swing to her step and discovered that being well-grounded through her feet helped support her shoulders and head. She learned a series of gentle movements to open and rebalance her shoulders, explored some new options for her tennis swing, and all the different reachings that were so much a part of her job as a housekeeper. In her last session she reviewed all the movements she had learned to assist her in her opening process, and we wove them together into a sequence she could use on her own.

I talked to Jocelyn recently, eight months after her last session. She seems taller than before her movement work, breathes more freely, carries her head up most of the time, and feels more open to other people. Although from the very beginning she found dynamic balance more comfortable, at first it was difficult to maintain because of its strangeness. Now she spends most of her time well supported without thinking much about it. She still occasionally slips into an old pattern, but soon feels the stress of it and adjusts easily to regain support, the path between those two options now easy and familiar.

Just recently she is realizing that she has a brand new way of dealing with stress. Her breath is still the first thing to go when she gets upset, but now she notices it right away and doesn't have to have an asthma attack to call it to her attention. Her old way of handling stress, which she is just now becoming aware of, was to stop breathing, make herself very small, withdraw, and get sick. All of these actions combined to make her incapable of dealing with the source of the difficulty. Now, when angered or threatened, she consciously takes a breath, which makes her feel bigger and better able to cope with the situation.

She is sick less frequently and feels stronger under stress. She feels that her new stance and her new breathing patterns are important parts of her more powerful way of being in the world.

APPENDIX C
Exercises for Integrated Development

Dr. Rolf's Elementary Structural Patterning Exercises

This sequence of movements helps to reinforce patterns established by the Rolfing work. These movements will give you an experience of internal order, starting from the legs and progressing to the neck. The sequence begins with the body out of gravity (sitting and lying down) and progresses to experiencing gravity while standing and moving. Although the sequence is presented as a package, any portion of it may be practiced separately to pattern order and balance into a specific area of the body.

Exercise I — The Arch Builder

This is an excellent set of movements designed to create an arch in flat feet and to generally strengthen the ankles and arches of any foot type.

Sit with your back against a wall and your legs extended straight in front of you. Keep your low back against the wall during the whole sequence and do not release the legs until the sequence is completed. The legs are kept together with knees and ankle bones touching at the inner surface if possible. Most people have a hard time doing this so don't strain. (The drawings will show the feet slightly apart. (Figures A1,2,3,4) Point the toes down and the feet down at the ankle joint. Keep toes and feet in this position and begin turning the whole leg out from the hip joint as far as it will go, then return to the starting position very slowly. Initiate the return movement from the internal ankle bone. (Figures B5 and 6) Keep the foot down at the ankle and just turn the toes up. Repeat the turnout pattern and focus on the hip, as the place where the turning starts from. Return to the starting position while focusing on the inner ankle. (Figures C.7 and 8) With the toes still up, bring the foot up at the ankle, extending the heel as far as you can. (Remember to keep your back and buttocks flat against the wall.) Again, turn out from the hip and slowly roll the leg back in, leading with the inner ankle bones. Now the sequence reverses itself. Foot down with toes up, turning out from the hip, in at the ankle. Toes down, foot down — and then relax. Do both legs together, then one leg at a time. To review — A. Toes down, ankle down. B. Toes up, ankles down. C. Toes up, ankle up, then reverse. D. Foot down, toes up, back to E. Starting point — Toes down, ankle down.

For extremely flat feet do these twice a day when you get up and before you go to bed. As a general strengthener, perform the sequence once a day until you feel that your feet and ankles have improved to your satisfaction.

FIGURE A1   Feet Neutral   **Starting Position**

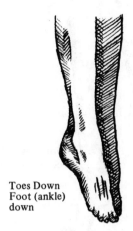

Toes Down
Foot (ankle)
down

FIGURE A2

Side View / Starting and
ending position

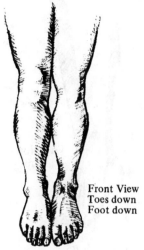

Front View
Toes down
Foot down

FIGURE A3

Starting and ending
position

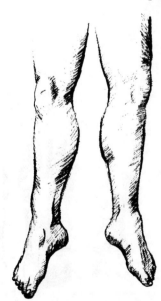

Foot down
Toes down

Legs turned out

FIGURE A4

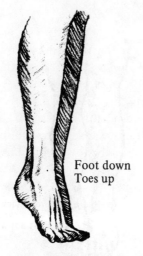

Foot down
Toes up

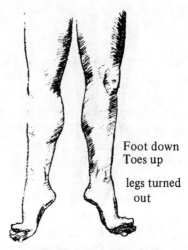

Foot down
Toes up

legs turned
out

FIGURE B5   Side View
starting and ending position

FIGURE B6   Front View

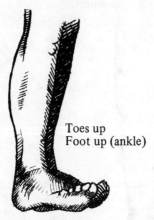

Toes up
Foot up (ankle)

FIGURE C7
Side View
Starting and ending
position

Toes up / legs turned out
Foot (ankle) up

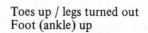

FIGURE C8   Front View

Exercise II — Leg and Hip Patterning

This exercise will relieve low back tension. Lie on your back with your legs straight, arms along your sides, palms down. (Figure A9) Slowly bend and raise your right knee as if it were being lifted by a string attached to the knee-cap. (Your heel pivots but does not slide. Figure B10) Keep moving until there is a flexion crease where the leg and groin connect. (Figure C11) Slowly lower the knee with the heel hitting first, then slide the foot down to the rest position. Try to stay long in the groin (don't let lower back arch up as you return the leg to the ground). Repeat this movement with the other leg. Do about five sequences of this pattern. This pattern helps to create a line of connected movement up through the legs and groin, to the front of the spine where some of the muscles used in the movement are located. The direction for this exercise is "straight forward, straight back" because the first movement of the knee should be straight toward the ceiling before the knee begins to arc headward.

Knee toward ceiling first
A

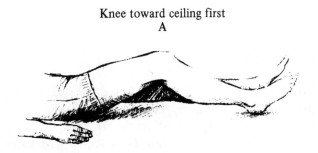

FIGURE A9

Knee moves straight up, straight forward,
(toward head) and straight back
(leg extended)
B

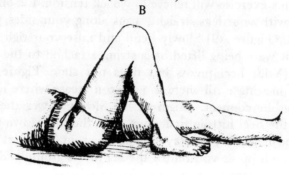

FIGURE B10

Heel slides foot to
resting position
C

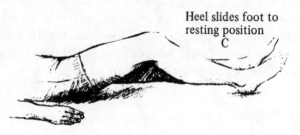

FIGURE C11

Exercise III — Pelvic Lift

This exercise will help to organize the relationship of
the pelvis to the hip joint and lower back.

Lie on your back as in Exercise II with the legs extended and palms down. Draw *both* legs up to form an
equilateral triangle. (Figure A12) Reach out with the
knees (keep them parallel in the direction indicated.)

This will lift and roll back the pelvis (with the tailbone leading the movement). (Figure B13) Continue this movement, lifting the pelvis and spine progressively until the weight rests between your shoulder blades. (It is essential that the lift comes from reaching with the knees rather than from flexing the stomach muscles. Put your hand on your belly to monitor this.) (Figure C14) Retrace this movement line, slowly coming back down as if laying a chain (your spine) out on the floor, link by link. (Figure D15) Some parts of the spine may come down on the floor stuck together. During the next repetition, try to get individual movement there. Repeat this 4-6 times, 3 times a week for general patterning, more often (daily) if you have specific problems in these areas.

Reach out with knees

FIGURE A12

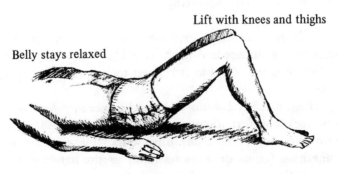

Lift with knees and thighs

Belly stays relaxed

FIGURE B13

Come down one vertebrae at a time

FIGURE C14

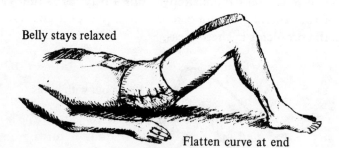

Belly stays relaxed

Flatten curve at end

FIGURE D15

Exercise IV — Arm Balancing

This exercise helps to improve the relationship of the arms to the ribcage and neck. It will aid in relieving some of the neck tension that is related to improper use of the arms.

(Figure A16) Lie on your back, knees up or down as low back comfort dictates, with arms spread out in line with the top of your armpits. Mark this position with something (coins or masking tape) as the hands must return to this point several times during the exercise. This is a "stress exercise", like the arch builder, so the arms should not be released until the sequence is completed. (Figure B17) With palms down, raise your arms straight up, bringing the back of the hands together and extended over your face. (Be aware of your shoulder blades. They should stay fairly flat on the floor while the arms move in the shoulder socket.) (Figures C18 and D19) If the blades start to raise up before the back of the hands touch, stop at that point. (Figure E20) Slowly return arms to original position (palms down) and without releasing the arm position, turn the arm ¼ so the thumbs point to the ceiling. (Focus the turning action at the shoulder rather than the forearm.) (Figure F21) Bring arms back to the up position and lower them slowly to starting position. Watch your breathing. Keep it smooth and relaxed. (Figure G22) Again rotate the arm (focusing on the shoulder) ¼ turn so that the palm now faces up. Repeat the up and down movements slowly. The arm rotates again ¼ turn so that the little finger is up and the movements are repeated. The sequence is repeated in reverse order by quarter turns from palm up, thumb down, to closing with palm down. (Figures H23, I24) After reaching the palm down position, sweep the hands down to your sides and rest. Feel the flatness of the shoulder blades on the floor, the softness of the arms in their sockets and the openness of the upper ribs and chest.

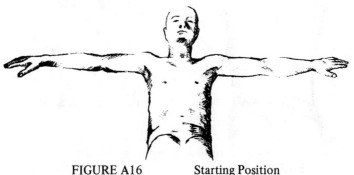

FIGURE A16   Starting Position

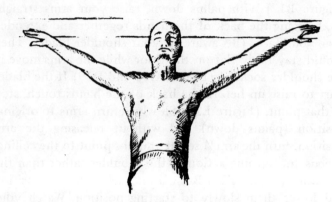

FIGURE B17

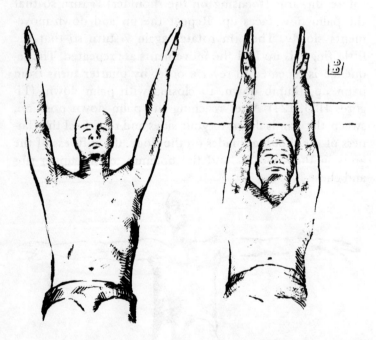

FIGURE C18   **FIGURE D19**

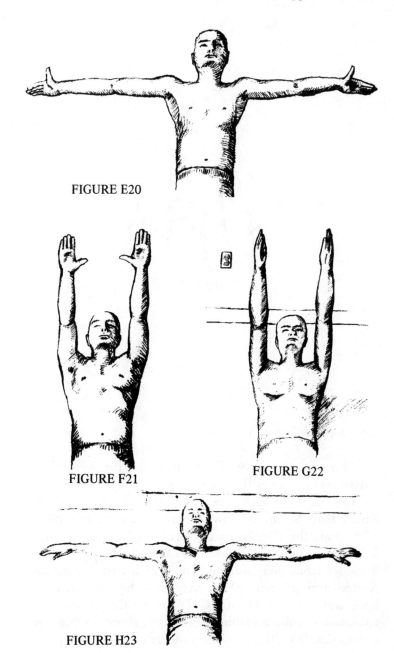

FIGURE E20

FIGURE F21

FIGURE G22

FIGURE H23

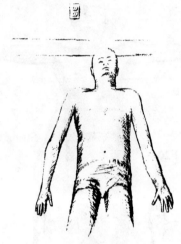

FIGURE I24

Exercise V — Elbow Movement

This exercise teaches the body to use the pectoral and latissimus muscles as the primary movers of the arm.

Lie on your back, arms at sides with palms down. Knees may be up or down as comfort dictates. (Figure A25) Slide the elbows straight out (both at the same time) and straight back in. (Figure B26) Move the arms only 4 to 8 inches from your sides or you will be using your pre-Rolfed arm pattern, which over-uses the deltoid, upper back and shoulder. (Figure C27) Repeat this movement 4 to 5 times while breathing peacefully. (Imagine you have strings *lightly* pulling on the tip of the elbow.)

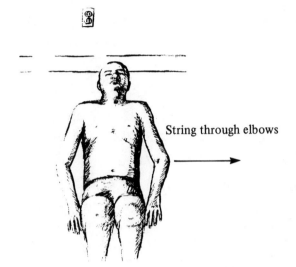

String through elbows

FIGURE A25

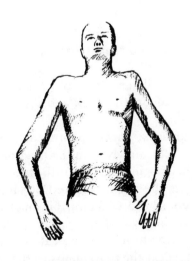

FIGURE B26

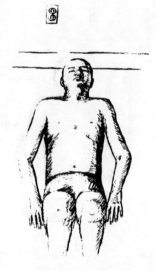

FIGURE C27

Exercise VI — Head and Neck Balancing

This exercise will give you the experience of gently balancing the head on the neck and the neck on the rib-cage.

Lie on your back, knees up, arms at sides with palms down. (Figure A28) Slowly turn the head to one side with the point of focus being the top of the head. (Figure B29) Don't shorten at the neck. (Figure C30) Imagine a string at the top of your head which runs through the mid-point of your head at the level of the ears, behind the nose. Let this imaginary string turn your head. Return to center, rest a moment and repeat the movements to the other side. Repeat three times in each direction.

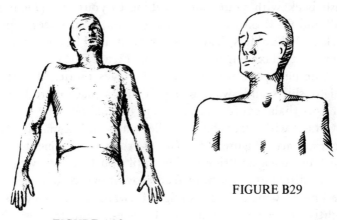

FIGURE B29

FIGURE A28

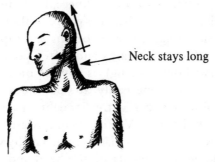

Neck stays long

FIGURE C30

Exercise VII – Integration

This segment puts the previous six exercises together, bringing balance and order to all the body's hinges and then experiencing them in movement.

From a prone position, draw your knees up and roll to your side. (Figure A31) Slowly push up to all fours and push back with your hands, rolling to your feet (Figures B32 and C33) Slowly uncurl (straighten) your knees, hips, back and shoulders, leaving your head until last, until you come to a relaxed upright position. (Figure D34)

The next part of this exercise involves a series of subtle weight shifts and swaying as you find a place of rest and comfort (balance) for each segment of the body.

Start with your feet parallel and approximately 12 inches apart. (Figure E35) Gently rock your weight forward and back and side-to-side until you feel your weight evenly distributed on both feet. Now move your focus to the knees, swinging them straight forward and back ever so slightly and evenly through both knees. Find the position where the knees are neither locked back or overly bent, but softly open. Now roll the pelvis forward and back around the hip joint. As with the knees, find the midpoint where the pelvis seems to balance easily without holding, to act as a basin to contain your organs and support your ribcage. Take a few full breaths and soften your shoulders so they ride (without holding) as a yoke on the ribcage. Allow your arms to hang easily at your sides and move your elbows slowly and slightly, straight in and straight out 5 times, as in Exercise V. Focus your awareness on the head and allow it to find its place of balance by very small "yes-no" nodding movements of the head and neck. The eyes should be soft as if not quite focused on something way in the distance. Return your awareness to your ankles and sway back and forth through this joint, feeling weight move from the ball of the foot back to the heels and forward to the toes. Allow the swaying to progress upward through the knee, hip, chest/shoulders and neck hinges. Imagine the top of your head gently lengthening as you sway forward and allow your spine to pull you on the backward sway. Try to find the place of balance "between the sways." (Figure F36) On one of your forward sways exaggerate a little bit and allow the momentum to carry you into walking. Enjoy the feeling of integration and balance as all of your body parts participate together in coordinated movement.

Do this sequence at least 3 times a week. You can also vary the speed of the forward and backward swaying movements at times, to give you a different sensation of integrated movement.

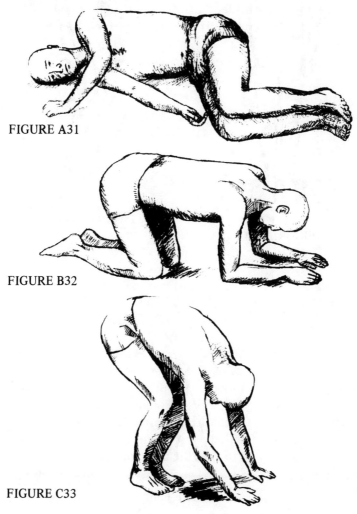

FIGURE A31

FIGURE B32

FIGURE C33

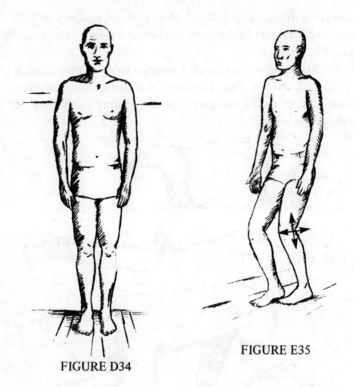

FIGURE D34

FIGURE E35

FIGURE F36

Basic Ten

These exercises are primarily keyed to the goals and body regions of the basic 1-10 sequence of Rolfing sessions. These exercises will be especially beneficial to anyone undergoing, or who has already received, a series of Rolfing sessions. Of course these exercises will be very helpful to anyone who wishes to improve the alignment and awareness of their body. (Some of these exercises are modifications of sequences from a Tibetan system of body electronics which is not discussed in this book.)[1]

Activity I — Full Lung Breathing

Stand with your back to the North in a fencer's lunge position so that the achilles tendon and calf of the back leg are well stretched. Place your hands flat on the top of your head, right first and left on top. Flex your elbows together and apart (touching in front) as fast as you can, inhale with elbows coming together and exhale with elbows coming apart. (Figure 37A,B) After every fifth complete elbow pattern (in front and behind) quickly change the position of your feet in a jumping/lunging action, remembering to exert a good stretch of the back of the (rear leg's) knee, calf and achilles tendon. Continue alternating legs every five repetitions until you've completed 50 sets. (5 breaths per leg position = 1 set.) Remember as you inhale to fill out the front, back, and both sides of your ribs (bellows breathing) each time.

---

1.   For further information on this system of body electronics contact the author at 1620 Cornell Drive S.E., Albuquerque, N.M. 87106.

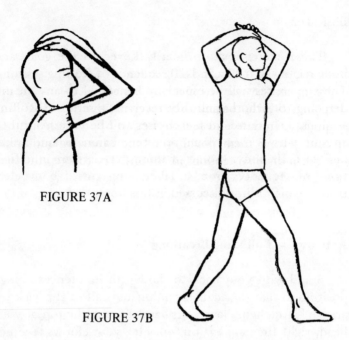

FIGURE 37A

FIGURE 37B

Activity II — Hinging Toes, Foot, Ankle, and Knees

A. Stand with feet shoulder width apart, knees bent, with both feet on seven layers of white typing paper, with back to north, one foot 4-6 inches in front of the other (bare feet). Curl your toes over a tennis ball, keep the toes spread wide and grip as if you're trying to pick the ball up with your toes. (Figure 38) Make sure your knee is centered over a point between the first two toes then bend your knee slightly and press your weight forward and into the ball. You should see the bones just before the toes ("knuckle up") raise slightly toward you. Hold this position for 15 seconds, repeat 3 times for each foot. Make sure your foot doesn't fall off to one side or the other by keeping the knee centered over the ball of the foot.

B. Imagine your toes to be fingers playing the keys on a piano. Try to "Play the scales" with your toes by lifting them up and setting them down flat one at a time, going from big to little toe and then reversing that direction fairly quickly. Initiate and feel the action of pulling your toes up and setting them down from the lower leg and ankle (see the individual tendons in action). Try to keep the toes spread apart. Most people have trouble with the last two toes acting as a unit instead of working independently. Stay with it and you will be successful. This is a great exercise when your legs and feet are tired. It will invigorate you and balance and strengthen your feet, ankles and lower legs.

C. If time permits you may also wish to include the integration exercise on page 241 which works on balancing the hinging and tracking action of your feet, ankles and knees. Do these in *super* slow motion to really feel the individual hinging action.

FIGURE 38

Activity III — Side Lengthening

Sit down with soles of feet together, heels close to groin and knees as flat as possible without straining. If you have too much pull along the inner leg put pillows under your knees. Interlace your hands behind your head (keep the elbows wide and pulled back). Keep your torso centered over your pelvis (don't bend much at the waist). (Figure 39) Lower your left elbow to your left knee as far as it will go (without raising the right sit bone off the floor). At the same time press your right knee and outer thigh down toward the ground while pulling and reaching over your right ear with your right elbow (you should feel a real good stretch along your whole right side). Hold this position for 20 seconds, taking a complete breath cycle (in and out). On the inhale attempt to lightly lift the 10th,

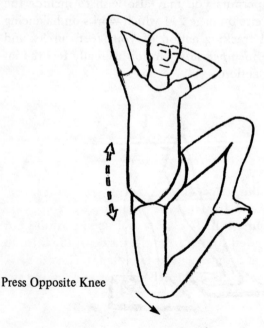

Press Opposite Knee

FIGURE 39

11th, and 12th ribs out, up and away. This should be repeated again on the same side then switch to the left side. Do five complete sets (two 20 second full breath cycles) per side. This will help to lengthen your torso and separate it from the hip where so many people are collapsed.

Activity IV — Groin and Pelvic Floor Flexibility

A. Sit with back to the north, soles of feet together and heels pulled up against the groin with knees as flat as possible, hands interlaced over toes. Roll your pelvis forward, keeping your back straight by pulling on your feet. Imagine you are attempting to roll your weight forward as in standing up. (Figure 40A) Inhale on the forward swing and exhale coming back. Again attempt to press the knees down and roll the inside of the thighs forward. Don't bend at the waist. On the forward swing imagine that you are sweeping your tailbone behind you and on the back swing (exhale) you are tucking your tail between your legs. As you imagine the lungs resting inside the pelvic basin, tighten your anus and pelvic floor muscles with the inhale (forward motion) and relax them with the exhale (backward motion). Repeat 5 times with eyes closed and really feel each opening and closing of the "breathing" inner pelvic bones.

B. Repeat this same action except you will spread your legs apart and flex the ankles up toward you as far as possible. (Figure 40B) (Not to a full open position but until you feel a good stretch from the inside of the knee to the groin.) Repeat 5 times with eyes closed, feeling the rolling motion in both the inner pelvic bones and around the hip sockets.

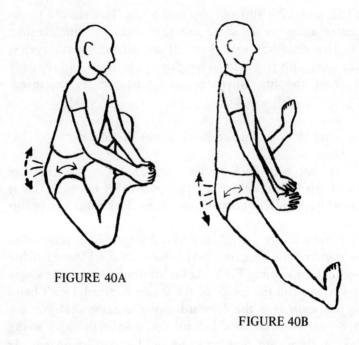

FIGURE 40A

FIGURE 40B

Activity V – Abdominal Release and Iliopsoas Activation

Lie on your back and draw left knee up toward your chest. Don't let the knee go out toward the shoulder, line it up closer to the sternum (breatbone) Your right leg is out straight. Begin sliding it along the ground (while inhaling into upper chest), drawing the heel until it clears the ground, keeping the knee nearer the body's midline. (Figures 41A-E) As the right knee comes all the way up to the chest, exhale, grab the right knee, drop the left foot (inner arch hits first) to the ground. As the foot hits exhale fully and fill out the lower belly wall (like blowing up a balloon) and flatten the lower back to the floor. Continue sliding the left foot all the way out until the leg is fully extended. Focus your attention along the inside of the foot, knee, leg, groin, and waist and reach from above with the iliopsoas to stretch your foot out. Just think of yourself trying to stamp out a cigarette but starting with the top of the leg attachments (deep in the lower belly wall) pushing all the way through the inside of the heel. Continue this alternating pattern for 25 repetitions of each leg.

FIGURE 41A

FIGURE 41B

FIGURE 41C

FIGURE 41D

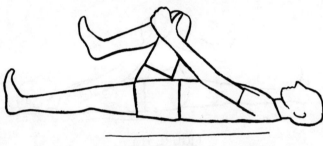

FIGURE 41E

Activity VI – Low Spine/Pelvis Articulation

A. Go on elbows and knees with head to the north.
Put thumbs (tips) touching under chin and index finger in
the ears. Elevate lower spine and sacrum toward ceiling
as you inhale and drop them down as you exhale in a
pumping action. Breathe through the nostrils. Repeat for
3 sets of 15-20 repetitions.

B. Stand with your back to the south, bend down low
at the waist with hands contacting the floor. Now keeping
your waist down and hands on the floor look up as far as
you can. Hold for 15 seconds with 1 long complete breath
cycle (inhale/exhale). (Visualize the tailbone lifting up to

the sky on inhale and tucking slightly between your legs on exhale.) As you look up push your buttocks and legs back until you feel a good stretch in your low back and hamstring muscles. Drop the head toward the floor and interlace hands behind neck (at the point where head and neck meet) and pull down gently and evenly to release the neck through one complete breath cycle. Repeat the whole sequence four times.

Activity VII – Neck and Jaw Release

A. Lie on your back with head to the south, legs arched up (knees bent), feet not touching. Place left hand on back of neck and right on top of left. Now create full expressiveness in your face, using as many muscles as possible. Bug the eyes out, open the jaw wide, stretch the nose and forehead up and out. Now stick the tongue way out as if you were trying to touch the ceiling, reach out from in front of the neck where the tongue attaches. Now make a very guttural "ah ah ah" sound. Hold the face position for 10 seconds. Repeat 5 times. After you complete the facial expression close your mouth and eyes and make a soft flutter with your lips, tongue and throat like a very quiet motor boat. Repeat 5 times for 20 seconds each. Continue holding the leg and hand position for another 2½ minutes. The whole exercise should last 5 minutes.

B. Now stand up with your back to the north. Put your right hand behind your back and grasp your wrist with left hand. (Figure 42) Pull hard and steady with your left hand and simultaneously begin pulling your head and neck to the left away from your right shoulder. Keep the head straight in line with the left shoulder as if you are trying to touch your left shoulder with your left ear. Continue pulling on the right hand and bend the head back the other way, right ear to right shoulder. Reverse this sequence by placing your left hand behind your back and grabbing your left wrist with your right hand. Repeat the two-way neck movements. Remember not to bend forward at the waist or neck and to inhale going to the side and exhale coming up. Repeat 5 times with each hand or as time permits.

FIGURE 42

Activity VIII — Shoulders, Arms and Neck

A. Sit with back to the north. Place right hand on top of head and left on top of right. Flex elbows together and apart; touch in front and bring back parallel with the ears. Remember to keep your low back pressed against the chair back. Exhale going forward and inhale coming back. Do three sets of one minute each.

B. Stand sideways to a wall more than an arm's length away. Flatten your hand against the wall and spread the fingers wide. (Figure 43) Push into the wall with your right arm while you pull away with your body at the waist. Continue this 2-way stretching action by reaching away with your head and neck and trying to touch the opposite shoulder (left) with the left ear. You should feel pulling up the bottom of the arm right into the armpit and under the shoulder blade right into the mid-spine between the blades.

C. Place a wooden chair with back facing south. Straddle chair facing south (your back is pointing to the north). (Figure 44) Place hands together on top of the chair in the middle. Now bend back and place your legs over the top on each side of your hands. Your buttocks should be flush against the back of the chair. Lean back until your arms are fully extended. You will feel pressure along your wrists, elbows, arms and shoulders. Hold your head straight and every 30 seconds let it drop back for 10 seconds, then return to straight position. Repeat this pattern for 7 minutes if possible. Then pull yourself up to sitting; don't let your hands release until both feet are back on the ground.

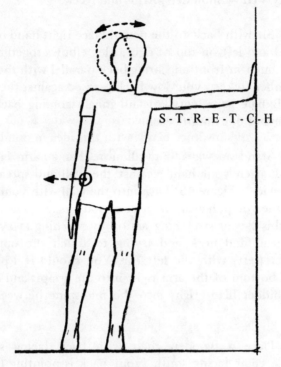

S-T-R-E-T-C-H

FIGURE 43

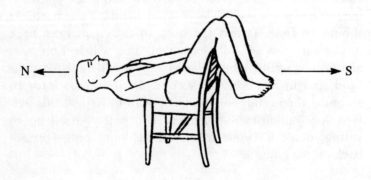

N   S

FIGURE 44

Activity IX – Hip, Knee and Ankle Integration

A. Stand with feet relatively parallel (slightly ducked out) approximately shoulder width apart. Imagine your legs to be like a water well and drop a coin (in your mind's eye) from the top to the bottom. If the hip, knee and ankle hinges are generally centered over each other the coin will drop straight through to the water (your feet). Do a series of slow knee bends with this idea in mind. Feel the interconnectedness of each of the joints, making sure the coin can drop all the way to the bottom. Evert (exaggerated duck out) the feet and do some more knee bends; pay attention to which parts of the leg are being worked. Now invert (exaggerated toe in) your feet and repeat the same bending action. Compare the two differing lines of muscle use (stress). Then return to a more normal (straighter) position and groove in the more comfortable and efficient pattern by doing 5 more knee bends.

B. Repeat the same bending action in each of the three positions (normal, exaggerated duck, exaggerated pigeon). Bend to your deepest position, inhale, hold a 10-second contraction (of the muscles), exhale, release the contraction and return to full standing. Repeat this sequence five times in each of the three positions.

Activity X – Spinal Balancing/Joint Rockers and Extenders

A. Lie on stomach, top of head pointing north, bottom of bare feet together, hands interlaced just below the collarbone on the breastbone with the palms facing inward (toward chest). (Figure 45A, 45B hand position) Hold this position 7 minutes. Your feet may be at any comfortable height as long as they don't touch the ground.

B. Stand with feet comfortably under you, lightly sway forward and back, bending slightly at the ankle, knee and hip hinges. On the fifth forward sway push up onto the ball (juncture of toes and foot) of your foot. Continue to lightly sway forward and back in this position. Feel the lift up through the ankle, knee and hip. Let the swaying motion carry upward through the pelvis and low back through the bottom of sternum (hinge), the arm and shoulder hinges, ending with neck and head hinges. Do five sways in this extended position, then on the 5th backward sway settle down onto your feet. Keep the lifted feeling in the hinges and keep the idea of the centered and lined up joints allowing the coin to fall through the plumb line as you sway ten more times. Be observant of where your body still resists allowing movement to flow through. Send a cleansing breath, as if you were taking a shower inside your body (allow the water to fall through the major [aligned] hinges), to those areas needing a little more movement. Continue slowing down the swaying movement until you are making the smallest movements possible. Now you are moving from the inside out as a pebble tossed into a smooth pond creates a series of waves from its center. Speed up and increase the swaying, then repeat the sequence, 5 flat footed, 5 extended, then 5 progressively slower flat footed sways. Come to rest after 5 sets of these (3 part) sequences.

C. Then go for a brief walk feeling the uplift, lightness, internal motion, and alignment of your body.

FIGURE 45A

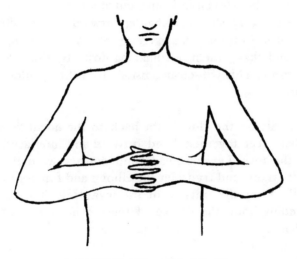

FIGURE 45B   Hand Position

Daily Unwinding (P.M.)

This short sequence will help you to release the pressure of your day, clear your mind, and help you to be well rested for the coming day. Some of these activities are modifications of a Tibetan system of electro-magnetic balancing which I use in my private practice.

1. Stand on 7 layers of stacked white typing paper with your back to the north, hands interlaced and resting on pubic bone, 3-12 minutes depending on how tired you are and how much you are on your feet during your workday. This will clear out fluids and blocked tension from the feet and legs.

2. Sit in a chair with back to the north, have right hand on top of head and left on top of right. Flex the elbows together (touch in front) and apart (return to parallel with ears) very slowly, exhaling forward and inhaling on the return. Continue this exercise for 1 minute. Drop your arms and shake them out hanging down by sides. Repeat once more. This will clear tension from the shoulders and the arms.

3. Sit on the floor with back to the north. Soles of the bare feet together, bend forward and interlace hands over the toes. Let the head bend down toward the toes (don't strain) and try to let the elbows and forearms touch the floor on the outside of the legs. Hold 3-5 minutes, depending upon the degree of tension in your neck and low back.

4. Lie on your back, head north, hands interlaced like a picket fence (crossing first knuckles) just below the breasts in center of chest, with the legs out straight 8-10 inches apart. (Figure 46A, B-hand position) Hold this position 5-20 minutes (no longer) depending upon your degree of mental and physical exhaustion.

You may choose to do any or all of these four releasing patterns depending upon how much time you have and any particular areas of your body that are tense at the time.

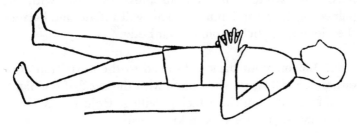

FIGURE 46A

FIGURE 46B   Hand Position

Daily Balancing and Energizing (A.M.)

This sequence will help to charge your body and balance its energy patterns before starting your day (or any time you need some energy).

1. Before you get out of bed (head pointing north), while still half asleep lying on your back, spread the legs apart and stretch the arms out wide. Hold for up to 10 minutes (at least 5 minutes). Then stand up with back to

north and stretch the arms up above the head with the palms together for 1 minute. This will inflate and balance the bio-electric field around your body.

2. Lie on your back with head to the north and arms outstretched toward the ceiling with the *back* of the hands interlaced and knuckles facing ceiling. Hold this position 3-5 minutes. (Figure 47A, B-knuckles)

3. Lie on your stomach, head to the north. Rest the chin on the interlaced hands (near base of thumbs) with palms together. Legs are out straight, 8-10 inches apart. Hold 3-5 minutes.

4. Stand with your back to the north; interlace hands over the belly button and flex arms against ribs rapidly 21 times, holding mouth open and panting as elbows hit sides. Repeat 3 times.

If you are short of time and need an energy boost just do number 2 for 5 minutes.

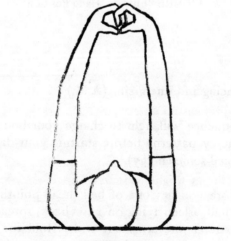

FIGURE 47A

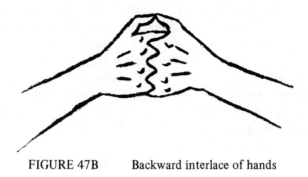

FIGURE 47B   Backward interlace of hands

Daily Back Care

These exercises will help to keep your low back and spine in good condition. If you develop an acute condition *do not* do these exercises and consult your "physician" of choice.

1. Go on elbows and knees with head to the north. Put thumbs along the chin and jaw (thumbs touching) and index fingers in the ears. Elevate lower spine and sacrum toward the ceiling as you inhale and drop them down as you exhale in a *pumping action*. Breathe through the nostrils and repeat 20 times.

2. Slow motion firming. Sit with your back pointing north. Legs are out straight and palms flat and resting on top of the upper thighs. (Figures 48A-E) Inhale and keeping your back straight slowly begin leaning back towards the floor, rolling down one vertebrae at a time. Once your head is resting on the floor the arms should extend out above your head as you exhale. Inhale and begin

lifting the legs (keep legs straight) and ankles flexed until the soles of your feet are pointing straight toward the ceiling. Exhale and lower the legs to the ground. As soon as the legs touch the ground begin raising the stretched-out arms and your torso up to a sitting position (inhaling). Once you reach the seated position begin exhaling as you drop the head to the knees and grab the toes with the hands. Slowly slide hands back along the thighs as you return to the sitting position. Try to do this as one continuous slow motion. Repeat the whole sequence five times.

3. Lie on your stomach with head to the north and bottom of bare feet together. Hands interlaced (thumbs touching) just below the collarbone on the breastbone with the palms pointing inward toward the chest. Hold 5 minutes. (See p. 259 Figure 45A,B)

4. Lie on back, head to north, left leg out straight. Draw right leg up, bent at knee and cradle the knee and lower leg in your hand) knee is pointing off to the side. (Figure 49) Keep the lower leg and foot straight. Pull leg and knee toward chest until you feel a good stretch along back of leg, buttocks and outer part of thigh. You should also feel a pull and light pressure at the joint between your sacrum and pelvis (illium). Inhale and exhale two complete cycles, then release the leg and do the same sequence to the opposite leg. Repeat 5 times for each leg.

Add the following exercises if you have been diagnosed as having scoliosis, lordosis, or kyphosis.

1. Go to a playground and find a bar or use a heavy chair or couch to hang by the waist (pillow or foam over bar; hold on to bar with hands or cross them in front of you). (Figure 50) Imagine a paintbrush attached to the top of the head and begin painting some figure-8 designs, first

horizontal and then vertical. Make sure you trace out the figure-8 pattern both from left to right and from right to left. Do five full figure-8 designs in each direction (left to right, right to left) in each of the patterns (vertical and horizontal). Feel the twisting action all the way down the spine to the sacrum. This will help to unwind the curvature patterns of your spine.

2. Lie on your back and draw your knees up. Begin a bicycling action, reaching out from the low back through the inside arch. Do five cycles forward, alternating legs (10 total), then reverse and do backward pedaling 5 cycles, alternating legs (10 total). *At the same time* slowly roll the neck from side to side in the following sequence. Right leg extended out away from the body, head turned to the left and eyes looking right. Return leg to neutral and head and eyes to center. At the same time extend left leg out and roll head to the right while eyes look far to the left. This will break down the neuro-muscular patterns holding the abnormal spinal curves in place.

3. Sit with your legs out in front of you with your back to the north, elbows resting on the knees, hands in a fist with thumbs resting under chin. Breathe deeply through the nose with the mouth shut. Hold 5-7 minutes. This will help to unwind the twists in your ribs and upper spine. Also make sure you do number 3 under "Daily Back Care."

Position A

Position B

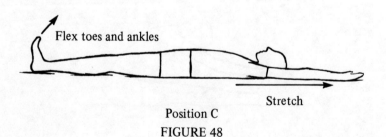

Flex toes and ankles

Stretch

Position C

FIGURE 48

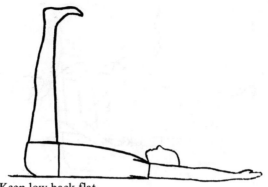

Keep low back flat

Position D

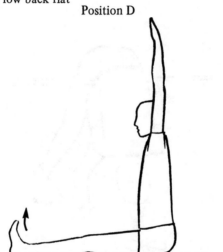

Position E

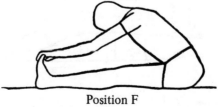

Position F

FIGURE 48

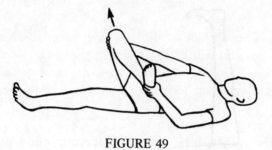

FIGURE 49

FIGURE 50

Tips for "Walkers," "Joggers," and "Runners"

The following ideas will help your running or walking movements and will help maintain the structural integrity of your body while improving performance, reducing injuries, and limiting long-term musculo-skeletal deterioration.

Begin with a brief scanning of your body position. Work with a partner in this exercise to get a more accurate picture of your body part locations. Let's start from the top and work down. 1) If something were balanced on top of your head, as you began to move would it be more likely to fall behind you (head tipped too far back) or in front of you (head tipped too far forward)? 2) Is the horizon line of your eyes seeing more of the sky or more of the ground? 3) Is the plane of your shoulders and arms predominantly resting behind or in front of your spine? 4) Is the plane of your sternum (measured at its bottom — xyphoid process) pointing more upward or downward? 5) Is the breastbone pushing more forward, causing the chest to wrap around behind you? Or is the breastbone kind of sunken, causing the ribcage and shoulders to wrap around in front of you like a heavy cape? Another way of measuring this is to ask "Is your breastbone in front of your chin or in back of your chin?" 6) Visualize your pelvis as a punchbowl. When you move are the contents more likely to fall on the front of your legs (pelvis tipped too far forward) or would they spill out over your buttocks and down the back of your legs (hamstring) — pelvis tilting backward behind you?

7) Now take a few steps and then look down at your knees. Are they tracking straight ahead or does one go off to the side, or does one point inward, crossing an imaginary midline? 8) How about the slant of your feet; are they hitting squarely on the ground or do they roll to the

outside (supinate) or fall toward the inside (pronate)?
9) Do you land evenly and move through the heel, ball and
toe portions of your foot, or do you land heavily on the
heel, or balance gingerly on the toes? There are much more
detailed levels of structural evaluation than this, but this
should be enough to give you lots to think about and learn
from your structure. Now that you have a greater awareness of your structure, the following information can be
applied to improve areas of alignment, efficiency, and responsiveness in your body as you jog or walk. I suggest
you choose 2-3 points to focus upon during any one time
you jog or walk until you feel a certain degree of comfort
and mastery with the ideas. Then you can move on and try
2-3 more until they all become part of your movement
style without you having to concentrate very hard on them.

   I.   Imagine a string or cable attached from your right
heel (middle of calcaneus bone) to the middle of your
right buttock. (Figure 51A) As leg swings forward and the
heel hits the ground your buttocks will be pulled forward
and down while at the same time lengthening your lower
back and spine. This should create a subtle and rhythmic
rolling action through your lumbar spine (low back) and
be carried down into your sacrum and pelvis. This light
swiveling action should help your weight line to fall more
toward the center of your foot. (Figure 51B) Imagine you
are riding a stationary bike; sit up high on the seat (i.e.
get your pelvis on top of your legs). (Figure 51C) Now you
can practice "running" in place by rolling the hips, knees
and ankles forward like 3 circles stacked on one another
(see drawing). Visualize the wheels of a locomotive train if
you are having trouble. (Figure 51D) Now practice reversing the action, like an exaggerated stationary "moon
walk" to groove in the most efficient line of transmitting
motion through these 3 major points.

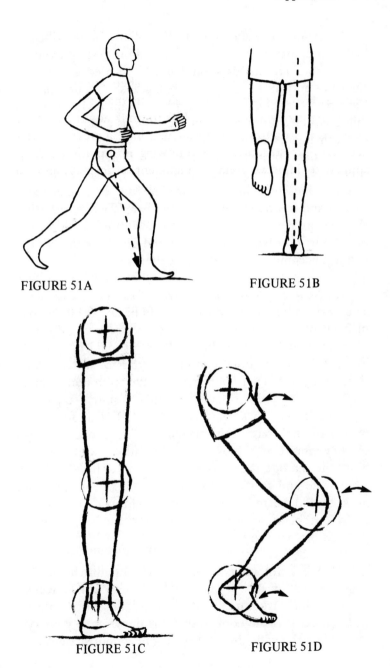

FIGURE 51A

FIGURE 51B

FIGURE 51C

FIGURE 51D

II. Allow your shoulders to float softly on the ribcage. Make sure that your shoulders and arms rest in front of your spine. The hands should not be carried any higher than the bottom of the ribs. The hands should not make a tight fist — let them flop like a loose pair of gloves. Maintain a contact point between the thumbs and index finger on each hand, making sure the bend at the elbow is no greater than 100 degrees. All of this will help you let your shoulders and arms glide along rather than be carried through muscular holding. Holding the ring finger and thumb and having the proper elbow angle will ensure that the accupressure breathing meridians running along the outer portion of the arm (tricep and crook of the elbow) will not become congested during your run.

III. Now let your focus move to the head and neck. The horizon line for your eyes should be about 30 feet out in front of you, not up toward the sky or looking down in front of your feet. The chin and teeth should float freely like a pair of dentures floating in a glass of water. Allow the lower jaw hinge to bob freely so the teeth don't touch. The eyes should also float softly and not stare — try blinking occasionally to keep them relaxed. Exhale forcefully on occasion through the relaxed mouth, chin and cheeks so they vibrate as if blowing bubbles under water, as you blow the air out the throat. The adam's apple should remain wide and flutter a bit as if gargling. The head and neck should be resilient, bobbing slightly in response to each foot plant as shock is absorbed and dispersed up through the structure.

IV. Now turn your attention to your ribcage and become aware of the "flow" of breathing as it traverses through your structure. First of all the nostrils should be wide (flared) as the cool fresh air is drawn into your system, down the wide throat, bringing new nourishment into the lungs. Visualize the ribs as a series of venetian blinds opening wide on inhale and closing on exhale as the respiratory assist muscles guide the ribs in their motion. You may wish to experiment with the number of strides per inhale/exhale cycle.[2] Remember to fill out as fully in the back and sides as you do in the front. As with a fireplace (bellows) the expansion should be nearly symmetrical and simultaneous in all directions (front, back, side-side). Feel the spine lift upwards and backwards away from the center of the ribcage. It is easy enough to feel the new air come in the nostrils, down the windpipe and into the lungs. For even more complete and relaxing breathing, try lifting the upper chest on inhale and allowing it to drop on exhale. Also allow the lower belly wall to fill up and kind of puff out during the exhale. This will bring a great cleansing and quieting feeling to your system as you run. In addition it will help to increase the volume of your exhale and keep you from holding too much air and energy in your upper chest (a common cause of arms being held too high and driving effort and strain into the neck). Visualize the breath being drawn up from the instep (arches) as a water bucket is pulled from the bottom of a well. This imaginary path should follow the line up the inside of the legs, through the inner aspect of the knee, up the groin and pelvic floor, following along both sides of the front of the spine, up the throat, straight up through the roof of the mouth right behind the nostrils, lightly brushing the eye sockets, clean out the top of the head. This breath path will keep the segments of your body connected, aligned, and give you a light, uplifted feeling as you run. Use it to invigorate yourself when you start to feel fatigued. Remember to allow your exhale to follow the same path in reverse, ending up all the way down at the inner arches.

2.   See Ian Jackson's *How To Breathe Better*, Doubleday, N.Y., N.Y., 1986.

So instead of tightening, gripping, and trying harder to push through your pain or fatigue, give yourself an internal energizing shower with fresh, re-oxygenated air flowing, uplifting and nourishing your body, *allowing* its natural strength to carry you through the tough spots. This ensures a more complete and balanced breath flow pattern with a body structure that is resilient and responsive to this major physiological and mechanical mechanism. The breathing rhythm indicates the degree of trapped anxiety and repressed feelings in a system. Running with balanced breathing can not only improve our distance and times but it may also contribute to releasing the neuro-muscular patterns which help lock in our mental and emotional stresses. Imagine a cable with a pulley attached at the middle of your sternum (breastbone). Feel yourself being pulled along this cable and with your arm movement you are basically pulling yourself in along the pulley, like reeling in a fish. This will also help to activate the strong psoas muscles while you are moving. If you wish to speed up for a short burst, you bend at the hips and allow the cable/pulley to lean forward slightly and you will find that your feet will reach out to meet you.

V. Now let's bring some awareness to the body from the waist down. Unless you have a severe anterior pelvis (Figure 52A), imagine a tail attached to the tip of your coccyx (tailbone) and let it float behind you; not up high, but just dangling along the ground a bit behind you. (Figure 52B) Never run with your "tail" tucked between your legs or it will tilt your pelvis off of horizontal and cause you to compensate with altering your knee lift and stride length. Imagine your pelvis as a swing seat and the two psoas muscles are the ropes of the swing which attach to the tree which is the front of your spine. (Figure 52C) In this way your legs and the pubis (swing seat) initiate movement from above at a point where the swing ropes

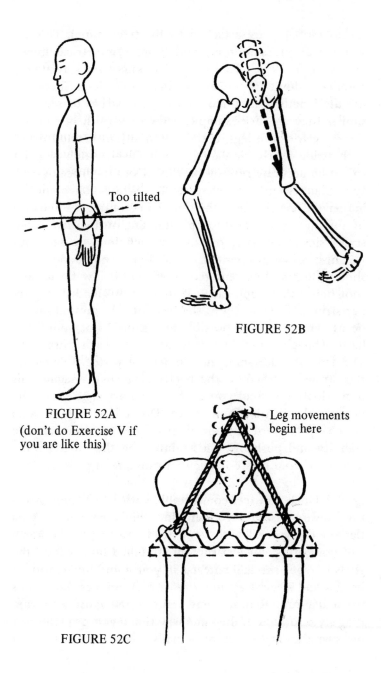

Too tilted

FIGURE 52A
(don't do Exercise V if
you are like this)

FIGURE 52B

Leg movements
begin here

FIGURE 52C

(psoas muscles) are attached to the tree (spine). This ensures stronger, smoother, and more symmetrical movements of the legs. Make sure your knees track relatively parallel — don't try and adjust them at the feet. Check the height, length, and force of each leg stride to see how similar they are. For example, is the knee lift height nearly the same for both legs, is the length, distance, and time of each stride nearly similar? (Have a friend watch you run to get an accurate reading on this.) Does the force of each foot plant seem somewhat similar or are you pounding harder on one side than the other? (You can get some idea of this in a static position by standing on two bathroom scales simultaneously, one under each foot, to see your weight-bearing differential.) The knee and ankle joints should float and be centered above and below the leg and foot bones they support, as if they are suspended on puppet strings. The contact of the feet with the ground should be as symmetrical as possible and should not pound too hard. (Imagine the feet laughing with each push off.) The front of the ankle should feel very soft. Remember the string attached to the heel (calcaneus), imagine this bone floating behind you as the string attached to the sits bones pulls lightly from above. Don't let the heel bone bunch up forward on foot plant or you will lose valuable stability and push off, thus reinforcing the inherent tendencies of your midfoot to either supinate or pronate.

VI. Once you feel comfortable with all of these structural awareness cues you should begin each run by lying flat on the ground with your head pointing to the north and your arms and feet slightly stretched out. Review the goals of your run and rehearse in your mind the important images and structural cues you wish to practice during this particular run. Rehearse and imprint the most ideal running style for you in the same way that a golf pro rehearses his swing mentally before actually doing it on the tee. If you do this before each run you will soon realize that you are running more purposefully (with mind-body integration), more efficiently (with biomechanical precision), and with a graceful and light feeling (fun). This will increase your enjoyment of running and decrease your likelihood of incurring injuries and deteriorating your musculoskeletal system over time.

VII.   End your run with a stretch routine that focuses on the areas of your body that you were aware of during your run. Then conclude with a Big Shake of your entire system, starting with your hands and arms, then let the movement continue up to your neck and down your trunk, through the pelvis and buttocks, doing one leg at a time (lift other leg off the ground) and shake the tension right out through the knee joint into the lower leg and ankle and out the bottom of the foot until you feel like a "wet noodle." The end result is a body grounded in ease, understanding, and quiet strength — The Power of Balance!

BIBLIOGRAPHY

Airola, Paavo, *Are You Confused?* Health Plus, Publishers, P.O. Box 22001, Phoenix, Arizona, 85028, 1971.

———*How To Get Well,* Health Plus, Publishers, P.O. Box 22001, Phoenix, Arizona, 85028.

Allen, Dorothy and Fahey, Brian, *Being Human in Sport,* Lea and Febiger, Philadelphia, 1977.

Anderson, Bob, *Stretching,* P.O. Box 1002, Englewood, Colorado, 80110, 1975.

Bailey, Covert, *Fit or Fat,* Houghton Mifflin, Boston, 1978.

Beiler, Henry M.D. *Food Is Your Best Medicine,* Vintage Books, N.Y., 1965.

Berrett-Rosannes, Marilyn, *Do You Really Need Eyeglasses?* Hart, N.Y., 1974.

Bertherat, Therese, and Bernstein, Carol, *The Body Has Its Reasons,* Pantheon, N.Y., 1977.

Brewer, Gail Sforza and Brewer, Tom, *What Every Pregnant Woman Should Know: The Truth About Diet and Drugs in Pregnancy,* Random House, N.Y., 1977.

Cayce, Hugh Lynn, *Faces of Fear,* Harper and Row, San Francisco, 1980.

Cohen, Bonnie Bainbridge, "Monographs on developmental patterning, endocrine gland processing and alignment." The School for Body/Mind Centering, 189 Pondview Dr., Amherst, MA, 01002.

Deutsch, Ronald M. *The Key to Feminine Response in Marriage,* Ballantine Books, N.Y., 1968.

Diamond, Harvey and Marilyn, *Fit for Life,* Warner Books, N.Y., 1985.

Dufty, William, *Sugar Blues*, Warner Books, N.Y., 1975.

Dunbar, Dr. H. F., *Emotions and Bodily Changes*, Columbia University Press, N.Y.

Feitis, Rosemary, *Ida Rolf Talks About Rolfing and Physical Reality*, Harper and Row, N.Y., 1978.

Feldenkrais, Moshe, *Body and Mature Behavior*, International Universities Press, 1950.

_____*Awareness Through Movement*, Harper and Row, N.Y., 1972.

Ferguson, Marilyn, *The Aquarian Conspiracy*, J.P. Tarcher, Los Angeles, 1980.

Gelb, Harold D.M.D., *Clinical Management of Head, Neck and TMJ Pain and Dysfunction*, W. B. Saunders, 1977.

Goldthwait, Joel M.D., *Body Mechanics*, J. P. Lippincott, Philadelphia, 1934.

Hanna, Thomas, *The Body of Life*, Alfred A. Knopf, Inc., N.Y. 1979.

Hunt, Valerie, "A Study of Structural Integration from Neuromuscular, Energy Field and Emotional Approaches", Dept. of Kinesiology, UCLA, 1977.

Huggins, Hal A. *Why Raise Ugly Kids?* Arlington House Publishers, Westport, Connecticut, 1981.

Johnson, Don. *The Protean Body*, Harper Colophon, N.Y., 1977.

Keleman, Stanley, *Your Body Speaks Its Mind*, Simon and Schuster, N.Y., 1975.

_____*Emotional Anatomy*, Center Press, Berkeley, CA., 1985.

Korzybski, Alfred, *Science and Sanity*, Edwards Bros., Inc., Ann Arbor, Michigan, 1978.

Le Boyer, Frederick M.D. *Birth Without Violence*, Alfred A. Knopf, N.Y., 1978.

_____ *Loving Hands: The Traditional Art of Baby Massage*, Alfred A. Knopf, N.Y., 1976.

Leonard, George, *The Silent Pulse*, E. P. Dutton, N.Y., 1978.

_____*The Ultimate Athlete*, Viking Press, N.Y., 1978.

Liedloff, Jean, *The Continuum Concept*, Warner Books, N.Y., 1977.

Lowen, Alexander M.D., *Bioenergetics*, Penguin Books, N.Y., 1975.

Magouin, Harold, *Osteopathy in The Cranial Field*, Cranial Academy, Journal Printing Co., Kirksville, MO, 1976.

McCamy, John and Presley, James, *Human Life Styling*, Harper and Row, N.Y., 1979.

Miller, Saul and JoAnne, *Food For Thought*, Prentice-Hall, N.J., 1979.

Montagu, Ashley, *Touching: The Human Significance of The Skin*, Columbia University Press, N.Y., 1971.

Murphy, Michael, *Golf in The Kingdom*, Viking Press, N.Y., 1972.

Oschman, James L. Ph.D., "The Connective Tissue and Myofascial Systems", The Marine Biological Laboratory, Woods Hole, MA, 92543, copyright Aspen Research Institute, 1981.

Price, Weston A., *Nutrition and Physical Degeneration*, Price-Pottenger Foundation, Inc., Santa Monica, CA, 1970.

Pritikin, Nathan, *The Pritikin Program for Diet and Exercise*, Bantam Books, N.Y., 1979.

Prudden, Bonnie, *Pain Erasure*, M. Evans and Co. Inc., N.Y., 1980.

Reich, Wilhelm, *Character Analysis,* translated by Theodore P. Wolfe, Orgone Institute Press, N.Y., 1945.

Rolf, Ida P. *Rolfing: The Integration of Human Structure,* Dennis Landman Publishers, Santa Monica, CA, 1977.

Roszak, Theodore, *Unfinished Animal,* Harper Colophon, N.Y., 1975.

Russell, Edward, *Design for Destiny,* Neville Spearman Ltd., London, 1971.

Sagan, Carl, *The Dragons of Eden,* Random House, N.Y., 1977.

Selye, Hans M.D., *The Stress of Life,* McGraw-Hill, N.Y., 1956.

Stoddard, Allen, *Manual of Osteopathic Technique,* Hutchinson of London, 1959.

Sweigard, Lulu, *Human Movement Potential,* Harper and Row, N.Y., 1974.

Thomas, Lewis, *The Lives of A Cell,* Bantam Books, N.Y., 1974.

Todd, Mabel, *The Thinking Body,* Dance Horizons Inc., Brooklyn, 1937.

Tompkins, Peter, *The Secret Life of Plants,* Harper and Row, N.Y., 1973.

Upledger, John, and Vredevoogd, Jon, *Craniosacral Therapy,* Eastland Press, Chicago, 1983.

Upledger, John, *Craniosacral Therapy II, Beyond The Dura,* Eastland Press, Seattle, 1987.

Vassi, Marco, *Lying Down — The Horizontal World View,* Capra Press, Santa Barbara, 1984.

Metamorphous Press

METAMORPHOUS PRESS is a publisher and distributor of books and other media providing resources for personal growth and positive changes. MPI publishes and distributes leading edge ideas that help people strengthen their unique talents and discover that we all create our own realities. Many of our titles have centered around NeuroLinguistic Programming (NLP). NLP is an exciting, practical and powerful model of human behavior and communication that has been able to connect observable patterns of behavior and communication to the processes that underlie them.

METAMORPHOUS PRESS provides selections in many subject areas such as communication, health and fitness, education, business and sales, therapy, selections for young persons, and other subjects of general and specific interest. Our products are available in fine bookstores around the world. Among our Distributors for North America are:

Baker & Taylor   The Distributors
Bookpeople   Inland Book Co.
New Leaf Distributors   Moving Books, Inc.
Pacific Pipeline

For those of you overseas, we are distributed by:
Airlift (UK, Western Europe)
Bewitched Books (Victoria, Australia)

New selections are added regularly and the availability and prices change so ask for a current catalog or to be put on our mailing list. If you have difficulty finding our products in your favorite store or if you prefer to order by mail we will be happy to make our books and other products available to you directly.

YOUR INVOLVEMENT WITH WHAT WE DO AND YOUR INTEREST IS ALWAYS WELCOME — please write to us at:

Metamorphous Press, Inc.
3249 N.W. 29th Avenue
P.O. Box 10616
Portland, Oregon 97210
(503) 228-4972

HEALTH AND FITNESS BOOKS
from Metamorphous Press, Inc.

Quantity

☐ **The Power of Balance**
A Rolfing View of Health

Brian W. Fahey, Ph.D.

This is a book about the importance of balance in all aspects of life. It expands upon the original ideas about improving health by balancing body structure first developed by Ida P. Rolf, Ph.D. Dr. Rolf developed a system of direct body manipulation and education known as Structural Integration, or "Rolfing." The Rolfing process educates, reorganizes, and balances the body into an integrated system. The balance achieved from Rolfing works its way through the whole system to improve our level of health. Rolfing ideas can be applied to all aspects of daily life, including how we sit, stand, walk, do our jobs, play, and ultimately, how we feel about ourselves. Reading this book can be a step toward achieving a high level of structural balance, energy, and well-being for yourself.
0-943920-52-3. . . . . Hardcover $19.95

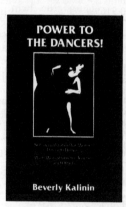

THE POWER OF BALANCE
A Rolfing View of Health
Brian W. Fahey, Ph.D.

☐ **Power To The Dancers!**

Beverly Kalinin

Power To The Dancers! is about the relationship between personal growth and dancing. Infinitely more than an exercise book, **Power To The Dancers!** adds dimensions to fitness by addressing the whole person. Author and teacher Beverly Kalinin shows how she discovered dancing to be the guide on her life journey and encourages others to do the same. Personal in nature, universal in appeal, the book is a chronological series of essays, poems, anecdotes, dreams, and observations on teaching dance, as well as detailed workshops on Improvisational Rock Dancing, Creative Dance, and Dance Yoga-Cize. The mood of this book is inspirational as well as instructive.
0-943920-44-2. . . . . Softcover $14.95

POWER TO THE DANCERS!

Beverly Kalinin

☐ **Your Balancing Act**
Discovering New Life Through
Five Dimensions of Wellness

Carolyn J. Taylor, R.N.

This intriguing new book in the field of Neuro-Linguistic Programming presents the systematic exercises and new material for changing the all important beliefs that underly the conditions that lead to wellness. Health, relationships, creativity, happiness and personal success are just some of the aspects of our lives that are effected by our beliefs, says Taylor. Recognizing that beliefs are a very powerful force in our behavior is the beginning of a process that can help us to create positive and productive results in virtually every capacity of life. Presented in an easily read and understood format, this book is a must for anyone who cares about their health or the quality of their life.
0-943920-75-2. . . . . Softcover $12.95

YOUR BALANCING ACT

Discovering New Life Through
Five Dimensions of Wellness
Carolyn J. Taylor, M.N.C.S.

Quantity

Fitness Without Stress
A Guide to The Alexander Technique
Robert M. Rickover

The Alexander Technique is today recognized to be one of the most sophisticated and powerful methods of personal transformation available. It has a long history of helping people improve their posture and coordination and it has proven to be an extraordinarily effective way to relieve stress-related conditions such as backache, depression, migraine, asthma and TMJ disorders. This fascinating method of achieving psychophysical well-being is fully described in this new book that can be enjoyed by readers with no previous experience as well as those who have already had lessons.
0-943920-32-9. . . . . Hardcover $14.95

FITNESS WITHOUT STRESS
A GUIDE TO
THE ALEXANDER TECHNIQUE

by Robert M. Rickover

The Elusive Obvious
Moshe Feldenkrais

In both his individual, hands-on body work (Functional Integration) and his group classes (Awareness in Movement) the author guides clients to discover for themselves what normal or optimum movement feels like. This sensing will then reprogram – his term is "rewire" – the brain accordingly.
0-916990-09-5. . . . . . Hardcover $19.95

The Master Moves
Moshe Feldenkrais

All Moshe's major ideas on movement, human development, sensitivity, awareness, and so forth are presented both as expositions and explorations through movement lessons. These lessons, part of his unique contribution to human development, are the key to understanding the Feldenkrais method. Use this book well and you will be surprised at the results.
0-916990-15-X . . . . . . Hardcover $14.95

Turn Your Pressure Valve Down
Richard Flint

Pressure demands understanding in order to turn it into a creative force. This book is designed to help with that understanding. It deals in practical realities with: understanding the value of pressure to your life; how pressure works in the human life; how pressure gains control of your life; and how to turn pressure into productive growth. It's more than just another book on stress management – it's a recipe filled with ingredients to make pressure the productive growth tool it was meant to be.
9-937851-22-1. . . . . . Softcover $10.00

METAMORPHOUS PRESS, INC.   P.O. 10616, Portland, OR 97210-0616

We accept Visa, MasterCard, Personal Checks, and Money Orders. Please remember to include $2.50 shipping and handling for the first book and $.75 for each additional book. Foreign orders, Air Mail, and UPS are subject to additional charges. Call **(503) 228-4972** to order by phone or to determine additional charges. Orders are shipped cheapest rate, unless otherwise specified. Book rate can take 3-4 weeks. UPS will deliver within 10 days depending on the distance from Portland. Prices and availability may change without notice.

Ship Via:

_____ Cheapest Rate

_____ UPS (add'l)

_____ Air Mail (add'l)

_____ VISA _____ MC

Total for Items $ _____

Shipping & Handling $ _____

Total Remittance $ _____

Exp. Date_____ / _____

Card No.:_____

Signature:_____

Name:_____
(Please Print)
Address:_____

City:_____ State_____ Zip_____